Farmhouse Kitchen
Freezer & Microwave

A sixth book of techniques and
recipes based on
the  Yorkshire Television series

Written by

MARIE EMMERSON

with a foreword by

GRACE MULLIGAN

Edited by MARY WATTS

YORKSHIRE
TELEVISION

First published in Great Britain, 1989, by
YORKSHIRE TELEVISION ENTERPRISES LTD
Television House, 32 Bedford Row, London WC1R 4HE

ISBN 0 946064 04 0

Design and production: Joy Langridge

Front cover illustration: *By the Farm Gate* by
Henry John Yeend King, courtesy of Fine Art Photographs
Back cover photograph: from Yorkshire Television by
Alan Harbour
Text illustrations *Food and Drink Collection* and *1800 Woodcuts*
both published by Dover Publications.

Printed in Great Britain by
Richard Clay Ltd, Bungay, Suffolk

CONTENTS

ACKNOWLEDGMENTS

Today, most of us cannot manage without our freezers and microwaves – but finding the kind of information and advice that helps to get the best out of both of them is not easy. I think you will find it in this book, which shows how to maximise the investment in these particular kitchen appliances to enhance your cooking and make the most of both your time and food budget.

Marie Emmerson has contributed valuable work to *Farmhouse Kitchen* in the past with her selection and conversion of recipes for the *Farmhouse Kitchen Microwave Cook Book*. This time she has taken on, with enormous energy, not only the development of new recipes but the preparation of an A to Z of freezing and thawing advice, and a most comprehensive assembly of information about freezing and microwaving techniques. These are all based on her years of involvement with domestic electrical appliances, and in particular the freezer and the microwave cooker.

In this book you will find masses of detail on using fresh and seasonal foods to stock the home freezer and, with the use of the microwave, to create some wonderful dishes for your family and friends.

Marie Emmerson has asked me to acknowledge with gratitude the help she has received from Vicky Andreas and Jeanette Shacklady.

Mary Watts

Autumn 1989

Farmhouse Kitchen is an independent production for Yorkshire Television made by Gaudy House Productions, and produced and directed by Mary and Graham Watts.

FOREWORD

If you happen to own both a microwave cooker *and* a freezer, you have two appliances which complement each other perfectly. Marie Emmerson has followed up the work she did on our first microwave book by setting out, in this latest one, every possible piece of information and advice to help you get the very best out of that magic partnership between freezing and microwaving. This pleases me very much. I am only too aware, while cooking on television, that there is never enough time to slip in all the hints and tips – and give all the advice – that I would like to; someone in the studio is usually giving me a signal to say: 'Hurry up, Grace! You're running out of time!'

I know you will appreciate the comprehensive alphabetical list which tells you how to pack and freeze everything with safety. It covers both raw and cooked food and gives detailed timings and instructions on thawing and cooking in a microwave. The hundred or more recipes which have been created for this book cover everything from soups and starters, through fish, poultry and game, beef, pork, lamb, rice and pasta, to vegetables, puddings and sauces.

This *Farmhouse Kitchen Freezer and Microwave* book will soon become an indispensable companion to our best-selling *Microwave Cook Book*. I look forward to using it on future programmes.

Grace Mulligan

CHAPTER 1

THE FREEZER

For centuries, people have found it essential to preserve food by using many methods such as salting, pickling and sun-drying. Using ice to preserve food is another ancient method and many 17th-century households had ice houses to do just that. However, not until the early 19th century did we see the possibilities of electrical refrigeration.

Freezing is the easiest, most natural way to preserve food and it is safe, because food-destroying bacteria will not multiply at very low temperatures. Food is packed and frozen at temperatures several degrees below 0°F/minus 18°C and then stored at just below that temperature. Most foods, if properly packed and frozen, can safely be kept for long periods. Food freezing is not difficult. In fact, it is very easy if a few simple rules about preparation and packaging are followed.

Most homes now have a freezer. In fact, the 1988 statistics show that there were freezers in 86% of the estimated 20 million homes in the United Kingdom, and microwave cookers in 46% of homes. It would appear that many people find that combining the freezer with the speed and convenience of the microwave cooker makes good sense for modern living.

Advantages of freezing food
Many advantages are given by preserving food in this way:

- It can be stored for very long periods without deterioration.
- 'Special' buys or economy packs can be bought when the price is right, then used up over several months.
- Cooking can be done when convenient, or when you are in the mood, and the dishes frozen until needed.
- Small portions and leftovers can be frozen, thus avoiding waste.
- Homegrown produce can be frozen for later use and any garden or allotment 'gluts' need not be wasted.
- 'Out of season' food is readily available to give variety to your daily menus.

Foods not suitable for freezing

Most foods and cooked dishes can be frozen and/or stored in a freezer and most electrical manufacturers provide useful information on this. Our A–Z section gives further detailed guidance. However, there are certain foods which toughen, separate, go limp, discolour or burst: so avoid freezing hard-boiled or scrambled eggs, milk puddings, aspic jelly, carbonated or fizzy drinks, custard, royal icing, raw salad vegetables with a high water content such as lettuce and cucumber, also bananas, some cheeses and types of cream, mayonnaise, and eggs in shells.

The types of freezer

In 1973 a special symbol was introduced for freezers [✳ ✳✳✳] to distinguish between those appliances designed for the storage of frozen foods and those designed to freeze as well as store them. This symbol was agreed by the International Standards Organisation and supplements the one, two or three-star classification system for the storage of commercially frozen foods. It is prominently and permanently marked on freezers. The weight of food which can be frozen in each cabinet without lowering the quality of already-frozen food is given in the freezer manufacturer's instructions and on the rating plate fixed to the freezer.

There are three basic cabinet shapes:
The chest type has a top-opening lid. Capacities range from about 100 litres upwards. Removable wire baskets or trays are essential for chest freezers, along with coloured bags so that foods may be packed and stored according to type. Finding what you want may otherwise become quite a problem.
The upright type, which usually takes up less floor space than the chest freezer, has a front-opening door. It used to be thought that every time you opened the door cold air tumbled out, which in turn led to a greater consumption of energy to cool the freezer down again. Current models however, are usually fitted with 'baffles' to lessen this and upright freezers are easier to pack and unpack than chest freezers, and stocks may be easily checked. Fittings include shelves, drawers and/or baskets which may slide in and out. Sizes are from 100 litres upwards but, for small families or small flats, there is also a 50-litre free-standing model that can be placed on top of a refrigerator or a work surface.
The fridge/freezer type combines a refrigerator and an upright freezer in one unit. The freezer section is designed to freeze fresh foods and store both these *and* commercially frozen foods for long

periods. The refrigerator section is designed to keep perishable food fresh for short periods by keeping its temperature below 47°F/7°C.

IMPORTANT: **Evaporators** (the technical name for the frozen food storage compartment in a refrigerator) are designed to store *pre-frozen* food, *not to freeze food.* Commercially packed frozen food will indicate by a star rating how long it may safely be stored in an evaporator. The evaporator will display the corresponding star marking:

* the frozen food storage compartment has a temperature of below 21°F/minus 6°C.
** the frozen food storage compartment has a temperature of below 10°F/minus 12°C. Frozen food can be kept for 1 month.
*** the frozen food storage compartment has a temperature of below 0°F/minus 18°C. Frozen food can be kept for 3 months.

It is important that all bought frozen foods are placed in the frozen food storage compartment (evaporator) as soon after purchase as possible and used within the stated time.

Installation
A freezer or a fridge-freezer needs no special installation as it can simply be plugged into a 13 amp socket outlet. Many people use a brightly coloured plug top to identify their freezer so that it is never unplugged by mistake, should other socket outlets be nearby.

A cool, dry and well-ventilated position is needed for siting a freezer or fridge-freezer. Should kitchen space be limited, it may be convenient to find room in a corridor, spare room, under the stairs or even in a garage (provided this doesn't leak). Cool surroundings will mean less wear for the motor and less fuel consumption.

Controls
A freezer may be fitted with one or more controls and indicator lights and it is worth being aware of their uses. The manufacturer's instruction book should always be read and followed, but the following information may prove helpful:
The 'on/off' switch should always be switched off and the freezer unplugged before any cleaning operation is carried out.
The 'supply on' indicator light is there so that you can see at a glance that the appliance is plugged in and switched on.

A temperature warning light comes on when the cabinet is not at the correct cold temperature and the reason should be investigated at once. It may be that the lid or door has been left ajar and warmer air has entered, or that the temperature control dial needs to be readjusted.

The temperature control dial should not be set, then ignored. This dial ensures that the correct freezing temperatures are maintained. If the weather or perhaps the kitchen is very hot then the dial may need to be altered.

The 'fast freeze' switch *must* be used when freezing fresh food or cooked dishes, as it overrides the thermostat and ensures that the temperature is low enough to freeze the food without affecting the already-frozen food in storage. The manufacturer will recommend how long this switch must be kept on.

A 'fast-freeze' indicator light may be fitted to show at a glance from a distance that the fast-freeze switch is on.

Rules for packaging and freezing

It is important to read the freezer manufacturer's instruction book and follow any special instructions and details of control setting and freezing quantities that are specific to your model. Here are some simple general rules that are relevant to everyone:

- Before freezing food, set the control in your freezer in accordance with the manufacturer's instructions.
- Handle food as little as possible and keep it very clean.
- Freeze only food that is in perfect, fresh condition.
- Freeze food as soon as possible after gathering and/or preparation.
- Cool hot food quickly before freezing.
- Wrap food in moisture/vapour-proof materials.
- Always follow the rules and instructions for freezing, storing, thawing, reheating and cooking.

Food preparation and freezing techniques

To achieve best results, one of several processes is advised. These are detailed here and will be referred to in **bold** type throughout the A–Z section of this book. Most foods simply require careful wrapping to exclude air and for protection. Air inside a pack can cause discoloration, slows down the freezing process and dries out the food causing 'freezer burn'. This as well as being unsightly, may lead to the food being tough when it is cooked.

Meticulous labelling is essential.

Many vegetables require blanching, some fruits require freezing in sugar or a syrup, or may even be best frozen as a purée. Open-freezing is yet another process. Interleaving before wrapping certain foods (escalopes, pancakes) is a useful procedure.

Interleaving

This is used to prevent foods sticking together and being difficult to separate, a 450 g/1 lb pack of sausages for example. If you only need two or three, interleaving means you do not need to thaw and cook the whole bag-full. Suitable for chops, sausages, steaks, fillets of meat, fish and beefburgers.

Freezer polythene, greaseproof paper, foil or clear film can all be used; use a **double thickness** each time for the pieces of food to separate easily before thawing. If you intend to use the microwave for thawing or cooking, then **foil must not be used**.

Open-freezing

A useful alternative to interleaving for large quantities of chops, sausages, fish fillets or chicken joints; also for blanched vegetables and whole fruits which, if packed together before freezing, will stick together. Useful, too, if you need to go to the freezer for just one or two items or for 'free-flowing' fruit and vegetables; and it makes packing easier.

How long does it take? The time depends on several factors, including the type of food, its temperature before freezing (room or refrigeration), the density, the quantity and its actual size.

Many freezer manufacturers suggest open-freezing overnight; this is based on the *maximum* quantity of food which can be frozen from fresh at any one time. (Check with the manufacturer's instruction book, whose recommendations should always be followed.) However, when freezing smaller quantities of fresh food, follow this guideline: Lay the pieces out on trays in the freezer. For 250 g/8 oz of soft fruit, allow about $2\frac{1}{2}$ hours; for the same quantity of vegetables, about 3 hours; for two whole fish such as trout, four thick sausages, four chops or poultry pieces allow 3 to 4 hours.

Although a covering is not usually required, it is best to cover meat or poultry with clear film as this gives added protection against 'freezer burn', especially in the thinner areas.

Pack open-frozen food straight into large, strong bags labelled with date, etc. Do not mix up batches frozen on different dates. Here, however, is a word of caution about open-freezing, especially for meat, poultry and fish if left for any length of time before packing into bags: The longer it remains exposed, the more likely it is to dehydrate and possibly suffer 'freezer burn'. Likewise, the colour may deteriorate and the food can toughen.

Fruit preparation
Fruit may be frozen in one of several ways, depending upon its type and your requirements. The A–Z section which follows (page 27) indicates in **bold** type which of the following methods to use:

1 **In dry sugar**
Use approximately 125 g/4 oz caster sugar per 450 g/1 lb fruit. Turn the fruit gently in sugar until evenly coated. Pack in plastic containers, leaving 2 cm/$\frac{3}{4}$ inch headspace (space below the rim of the container for the fruit and sugar to expand).

2 **In sugar syrup**
Make syrup using 225 g to 450 g/8 oz to 1 lb per 600 ml/1 pint of hot water. Dissolve the sugar in the water, stirring constantly over low heat, then bring to the boil for a minute or two. Allow syrup to get quite cold. Make sure the fruit is covered with syrup, but allow 2 cm/$\frac{3}{4}$ inch headspace below the lid of the container because the contents expand as they freeze. To help keep the fruit beneath the syrup, pack crumpled waxed or greaseproof paper over it, so when the lid is on, it presses the fruit down.

3 **Open-freezing**
Spread prepared fruit on trays or plates, without sugar, and freeze overnight. Then pack and store in boxes.

4 **As a purée**
Purée raw or stewed fruit in a food processor or liquidiser, or pass through a sieve. Sweeten to taste and freeze in small quantities.

5 **Stewed or poached fruit**
This freezes well, but remember to leave headspace for expansion.

Vegetable preparation
Many vegetables should be blanched before freezing as this retards the action of enzymes which otherwise can spoil both colour and flavour. The A–Z section indicates whether blanching is recommended.

Conventional blanching

A large pan is needed, big enough to hold 3 to 4 litres/5 to 7 pints of boiling water, with room to spare. Only 450 g/1 lb of vegetables should be put into the water at a time, but the same blanching water may be used for 6 to 7 consecutive batches. It should be returned to the boil between each blanching.

Have ready another large container of ice-cold water. (A plentiful supply of ice made overnight in the freezer helps to keep this water very cold.)

A blanching basket is useful. Lower each 450 g/1 lb prepared vegetables in the basket into the fast-boiling water. Time the blanching from the moment the water returns to the boil. (Detailed information on preparation and timing is given in the A–Z section.) Transfer the basket of vegetables to the ice-cold water, allowing plenty of room for them to circulate in the water. Lift the vegetables out to drain, pack them into containers, and freeze. Or pat dry between kitchen paper towels and then open-freeze: Spread on trays and freeze overnight, then pack.

Microwave blanching

Should large quantities of vegetables need blanching, use the method given above. However, small quantities can be blanched successfully in the microwave. Always follow your microwave manufacturer's instructions for timing. Never blanch more than 450 g/1 lb vegetables at any one time.

Prepare the vegetables as for conventional blanching by peeling, dicing, slicing etc. (see the A–Z section). Rinse in cold water. Place the vegetables in a medium bowl, toss in 3 tablespoons water, then cover and blanch on Full power (100%) for 3 to 5 minutes, stirring halfway through the process. Small diced, sliced vegetables will only need the shorter time. Large pieces and/or dense-textured vegetables should be given the longer time. Leave the vegetables to stand for one minute.

Plunge them into iced water to cool. Drain, dry, pack, label and freeze. Or open-freeze as indicated under conventional blanching.

Freezer packaging materials

For best results, all food for freezing must be carefully wrapped. Food must be covered completely and as much air as possible excluded from the pack; an easy way of doing this for 'solid' foods is simply to squeeze out as much air as possible, or you can lower the plastic bag and its contents into a bowl of cold water and allow the pressure of the water against the pack to push the air out. A freezer suction pump can be bought from freezer accessory suppliers. Liquids and foods with lots of liquid (e.g. casseroles; fruit in syrup) expand as they freeze, so should be frozen in rigid containers and not filled to the top to allow for this expansion. This is called headspace. Some types of fruit will be so light that it floats to the surface of the syrup. To avoid discoloration by exposure to air, pack crumpled waxed or greaseproof paper over the fruit up to the level of the lid.

Containers and wrapping materials

Packaging for the microwave: When the food is likely to be thawed, heated or cooked in the microwave, select packaging materials or containers that are not made of – or trimmed with – metal and are not likely to melt or distort with the heat of the food. Beware, too, of using wire ties covered with plastic or paper.

Bags: Freezer polythene bags are suitable for most foods, especially for moulding tightly over irregular shapes such as whole chickens or legs of lamb. They are also useful for liquids: First place the bag inside a rigid container, add the liquid, freeze, then lift out the bag, seal it and use the container again. It is worthwhile remembering to use strong bags if you intend taking packs from freezer to microwave for thawing and reheating or cooking. 'Boil-in-bags' are made of a special strong polythene or nylon material in which food such as stews may be frozen and reheated by boiling after freezing. Microwave boil-in-bags have plastic ties, not metal ones. They are also useful for freezer-to-microwave thawing, reheating and, in some cases, cooking. Laminated foil and plastic bags are leak-proof and good for storing liquids and semi-liquid food.

Cardboard: Wax-coated cardboard tubs should be lined with a plastic bag or foil, especially if they have been used before, and washed in hot water. If the wax coating has been partially removed by washing, the tub may be absorbent and even disintegrate into the food during thawing.

Foil dishes: Shaped aluminium foil dishes are useful for freezing pies, puddings, cakes and individual meals. They are light, space-saving and re-usable. The contents should be covered with foil and the whole dish enclosed in a plastic bag. Some types have their own

14

foil-covered cardboard lids and need not be wrapped. But remember that foil dishes cannot go straight from freezer to microwave cooker.

Polythene/plastic boxes: Rigid or flexible containers of various sizes with well-fitting lids are suitable for liquids, fruit, vegetables, cooked foods, sauces and fragile cakes. No sealing is necessary when a close-fitting snap-on plastic lid is used on a polythene container. Freezer tape will seal less well-fitting lids.

Underwraps and interleaving: Chops or other small pieces of meat should be separated and interleaved with two layers – or one fold – of freezer paper, foil or clear plastic film. You can then easily take out the number of frozen pieces that you want and even if you need a large number, it will take less time to thaw individual even-sized packages than a large number stuck together in one unwieldy lump. Sharp edges such as chicken legs should be padded with several extra thicknesses of paper or foil to prevent them piercing the outer wrap.

Over-wraps for polythene bags: It is wise to over-wrap bags containing large items with freezer paper or ordinary brown paper as this prevents tears in the plastic through friction between packages when the freezer is full.

Sealing aids: Sealing the bags, containers or wrapping is essential to ensure that the food is not exposed to air. There are several methods: A tight-fitting container lid will not generally require additional sealing, but take care when removing it as the material easily cracks in its frozen state.
Plastic or paper-covered wire ties or elastic bands can be used for closing the bags and freezer sealing tape for sealing edges of boxes and for keeping packages neat and secure. Ordinary adhesive tape *will not hold* at low temperatures.

You can also heat-seal, and some people even do this with the edge of their electric iron on its coolest setting – but you must protect both iron and plastic wrapping with two layers of tissue paper or iron and wrapping will suffer. If you seal near the top of the bag, it may be cut off when you come to unpack its contents and the bag can be used again.

Labels
The labels should give all the relevant information such as the type of food or dish, how many it serves or the weight, the 'use by' date

and, with experience, brief microwave thawing and/or cooking instructions.

It is a help to use different coloured labels for different groups of foods or store packs of similar foods in bags of different colours. Use a wax crayon, pencil, ballpoint or felt tip pen for writing labels. Ordinary ink tends to run and wipes off too easily.

Even the best adhesive labels can curl and fall off and leave you with surprises when a package you were *certain* was a prepared dish for an unannounced dinner guest turns out to be an uncooked ox tongue! The label can often be placed on the food itself *inside* the bag where it can always be read; or, if that is not possible, inside the neck of the bag near the tie.

Record book
It may be helpful to keep an 'in-and-out' record book of frozen food to use packs in correct rotation. Simply write down the 'date in', the name of the item and the 'use by' date.

Packing the freezer
The way food is packed inside the freezer is also important. Packages frozen into square or rectangular shapes will stack neatly in the freezer, using less space than round packages. Likewise slim, flat, evenly packed bags of frozen vegetables, cooked rice and pasta will thaw and reheat more successfully in the microwave than bulky or spherical packages. In chest freezers where it is all too easy for things to get confused, large coloured bags for different types of food are useful; green for vegetables, for example, blue for fish, red for meat, etc.

Defrosting a freezer
Moisture drawn from the air in the cabinet on to the surface of the walls and/or the shelves, freezes and creates ice. Most manufacturers give recommendations as to how frequently this should be removed to maintain the maximum efficiency of the freezer. Depending upon the type, this may be once or several times a year.

Defrosting can be a slow process but *under no circumstances* should another electrical appliance, such as a hairdryer, be used to speed up the thawing of the ice. The freezer should be switched off, disconnected, and the frozen food removed and wrapped in several thicknesses of paper (newspaper provides good insulation). Ice should be removed with a plastic spatula as the manufacturer instructs. Layers of newspaper placed in the bottom of the appliance helps to collect the ice or mop up defrosted water. Once clear of ice, the cabinet should be sponged down with warm water and dried.

Avoid using detergents as these may leave a smell within the cabinet. Switch on the cabinet and return the food as soon as a suitable temperature is reached

A recent innovation is the frost-free freezer which has an inbuilt method of keeping the inside of the cabinet free of ice and, as a result, requires no defrosting.

The freezer breakdown situation
The following information was prepared by the Electricity Council, and we are grateful to them for permitting it to be used here:

'The freezer is a very reliable appliance but should it be switched off inadvertently, the softening of food can be worrying. Don't panic! Even after considerably extended periods without electricity, all is not lost.

'Remember, frozen food takes a long time to thaw under normal circumstances so be aware that a loss of supply *for a few hours* will make very little difference to the state of food inside the freezer, especially when a large quantity of food is packed closely together. Unless several days' delay is involved, most of the contents of a freezer can be salvaged. All the food does *not* suddenly go bad. It will begin to thaw to normal, safe eating conditions quite slowly, at different rates according to kind, allowing time to deal with it. If a large quantity is involved, neighbours are usually willing to help store, or eat it. It is important to keep calm and to use your commonsense and knowledge of the signs of freshness in food to decide carefully which packs to keep, which to use straightaway, and which to discard. *If in any doubt at all* about an item of food, then discard it on the principle of being better safe than sorry.

'The chart on the next page may serve as a guideline, but the final decision has to be yours as you alone know the history of each item of food.'

TYPE OF FOOD	UP TO 8 HOURS FREEZER BREAK	UP TO 24 HOURS FREEZER BREAK
Fish Poultry Sausages Raw minced meat	If still hard, leave in freezer. Use within a few days.	If still hard, leave in freezer. Use within a few days. If thawed but still fresh, cook – or use in recipes – then return to freezer. Or cook and serve. Discard if in any doubt as to freshness.
Casseroles Stews Purées Soups and Sauces Other similar cooked dishes	These should stay in good condition. CHECK each item with care before using.	Some thick casseroles and stews may not have thawed at all. Keep in freezer and use as normal. Otherwise, eat at once. Thawed soups and sauces: reboil, then freeze. Use as soon as possible.
Uncooked joints and smaller cuts of meat	These should still be in perfect condition. Leave in freezer and use as normal	Should remain in perfect condition for 24 hours or more. If thawed, cook – or use in recipes – then return to freezer.
Raw fruits and raw vegetables	These should be in good condition, though soft fruits tend to collapse. Leave in freezer and use as normal.	Open-frozen fruit (packed) may collapse and no longer 'flow'. If still cold, re-pack into usable quantities and re-freeze. Fruit in syrup thaws fast, but may be re-frozen. Re-freeze vegetables if there is still ice on the packs. Otherwise cook at once.
Dairy Foods: Butter Cheese Eggs Cream and Yogurt	These should remain in perfect condition. Leave in freezer and use as normal.	Butter and cheese: Use as normal. Eggs, cream and yogurt: check and use at once – at discretion.

TYPE OF FOOD	UP TO 8 HOURS FREEZER BREAK	UP TO 24 HOURS FREEZER BREAK
Bread and Cakes Other baked goods	These should remain in perfect condition. Leave in freezer and use as normal.	All except cakes containing cream should stay in good condition. Re-freeze. Use cream cakes as soon as possible if cream is still fresh. Dairy produce deteriorates fast.
Pastry dishes	These should remain in good condition. Leave in freezer and use as normal.	Filled flans and plate pies: if pastry is soggy, discard. Cooked flan and pie cases, choux pastry cases: re-freeze and use as soon as possible. Uncooked pastry: cook, then re-freeze.
Ice cream Sorbets and Water Ices	If too soft to enjoy, discard. If not, eat at once. DO NOT RE-FREEZE.	Discard. Do not re-freeze.
Breadcrumbs Herbs	These should remain in perfect condition. Leave in freezer. Small quantities may be completely thawed. Use up as soon as possible.	Use as normal and as soon as possible.

CHAPTER 2

THE FREEZER – MICROWAVE PARTNERSHIP

The microwave cooker is probably most frequently used for thawing. Sadly, many people – after a few accidents – have not ventured wholeheartedly into cooking by microwave. With care and perseverence the results are good. But although the microwave cooker can be of tremendous benefit, it is unlikely to replace a conventional cooker which, for many operations like cooking very large quantities of food, will be more convenient and economical. Sometimes the results are better using the microwave for speed, then transferring the food to a conventional cooker to finish cooking and brown the food. By regarding the microwave as an adjunct to the conventional cooker, greater use can be made of both types of cooking.

The freezer has many advantages, but there are times when it is quicker to make the dish from scratch, rather than freezing, then thawing and heating in the microwave. Remember that the microwave cooker thaws and cooks not in seconds, but in minutes, and many dishes can be cooked in a shorter time than they take to thaw.

Power of your 'microwave'
Do you know what it is? If not, you will find it engraved on a small plate at the back or side along with other essential technical data. Otherwise, check with the manufacturer's handbook. The thawing and cooking times given throughout this book have been tested on a **700 watt** output cooker. Should your cooker have a lower output, a longer time may be needed. Check the food at the end of the stated time. If more time is required, allow:

about 10 seconds more per minute for a 650 watt output;
about 15 seconds more per minute for a 600 watt output;
about 20 seconds more per minute for a 500 watt output.

Timing
Some of the instructions in this book indicate thawing and cooking times, then continue 'or until tender'. As any cook will appreciate, the timings cannot take into account all the variables, such as the

age of the food, the size of your particular slices or dices, the shape of your freezer package, and of course the output of your cooker – if it is less than 700 watts. Although all the recipes have been tested, the times must not be regarded as *exact*. Microwave cooking is no more precise in that respect than conventional cooking, when one peeps and smells and prods and feels from time to time, to make sure all is well.

Food taken from the refrigerator will be colder than if it were at room temperature, so longer cooking time may be necessary. Different egg sizes will also give a different liquid ratio. The shape, size and material of the containers can also have an effect on the timing.

Like conventional thawing or cooking the result from 450 g/1 lb boiled potatoes will vary with the type used, the size, the temperature of the cold water, the amount of water used, the size of the pan and the wattage of the electric ring – or the pressure of your gas supply. Thus, when a recipe book says 'simmer for 25 minutes' it will rarely be *exactly* the same for everyone. Gradually you learn by experience how to get good results and, in some cases, what not to attempt to cook at all. For example, old woody vegetables will never be tenderised by the brief microwave cooking.

Containers and covers
As a general guide, the container capacities in this book are:

Large bowl	2.75 litres/4½ to 5 pints
Medium bowl	2 litres/3½ pints
Small bowl	1.5 litres/2 pints
Very small bowl	600 ml/1 pint
Large jug	1 litre/1½ pints
Small jug	600 ml/1 pint

The shallow dish will be dependent upon what you have in your kitchen and whether it fits into your microwave cooker.

When instructions are given to 'cover' food, a lid, plate, saucer or plastic film wrap (clear film) are all suitable.

Kitchen paper towel is generally used to prevent food splashing on to the walls of the cooker, or to absorb the fat or moisture from the food to stop it going soggy.

A note about clear film

Because of the recent research suggesting that there may be some health risks when using certain types of clingfilm, we have chosen to name it clear film in this book. You should choose to buy the brands that you are satisfied are not harmful.

If food is to be frozen and it is likely to be thawed, heated or cooked in the microwave later, it is important to give some thought to the packaging. Remember that metal in any form and foil (unless it is used in small quantities to slow down cooking by preventing microwaves reaching the food) cannot be used in the microwave. Also make sure the closure ties for bags are not made of wire, however well concealed. 'Arcing' and sparking are to be avoided always because they can damage the inside walls of the microwave.

Plastics must be able to withstand the heat of the food and not melt or distort. Some foods, such as vegetables or meat and fish in sauce, can be thawed in a 'boil-in-the-bag', but it should be pricked or left open to avoid a build-up of steam which might cause the bag to burst. 'Roast-bags' are also useful.

Labelling

This is important, as explained on page 15, but it is also useful if you can add simple thawing instructions so that anyone in the household can thaw or cook the food with the help of the microwave should *you* not be around to help.

A notebook

If you cook some foods frequently, it is worth keeping an alphabetical notebook with details of quantity, weight, microwave settings, approximate thawing, heating or cooking times for these.

Thawing foods

It is difficult to be precise about thawing times as these depend upon the output (wattage – see page 20) of the microwave cooker, the size and type of container, the age and quality of food and the sizes and shapes into which it has been prepared and packed for freezing. In some instances where food only needs thawing, the microwave cooker can be used to start the process, then only standing time is needed to complete it. Most manufacturers give detailed instructions and these should be followed as they apply directly to *your* microwave cooker. However, the following advice is important:

Once food has been thawed, it should always be treated like fresh food and used immediately.

If you intend freezing cooked fish and meat dishes *slightly undercook* them to allow for further cooking which takes place when the food is thawed and reheated.

Many foods such as hamburgers, sausages, fruit, vegetables, sauces, and cooked dishes, can be thawed on the highest power setting because they are small and thin and the microwaves penetrate throughout immediately. Thicker items, like joints of meat and poultry, thaw more evenly when you use the Defrost (30%) setting. The microwaves penetrate the first 4 to 5 cm/1½ to 2 inches, after which the thawing process continues by 'heat conduction'. On the Defrost setting, microwave energy is either pulsed or at a very low output (wattage) so that it does not go on to cook the part which has already thawed. If it is pulsed, the microwaves are sent out in bursts and the thaw gradually continues to penetrate the unthawed areas during the resting periods. Frozen vegetables can be thawed and cooked in one operation.

Fruits may need only a very short thawing time, but a long standing time to ensure that they do not over-soften.

Defrost (30%) is often the better setting to use with certain cakes, breads and pastries: for example a cream gâteau, Danish pastries or a loaf of bread. Full power could melt the cream, or draw out too much moisture from a loaf or cake so that it hardens to the point of being inedible.

Always ensure that large cuts of meat and whole birds are *completely thawed* before use. To ensure even thawing, it is advisable to start the process in the microwave but then allow the meat and poultry to stand until all the joints are flexible and no ice is apparent.

A standing time is frequently suggested by frozen food manufacturers. Apart from health and safety, it ensures the food does not start to cook in the parts where the ice has thawed, and it gives the remaining 'iced' area an opportunity to finish thawing out naturally.

You will find guidance in the A–Z and recipe chapters in this book, but always check and follow the manufacturer's instructions in your handbook or on food packages.

Generally, foods are covered when thawing to keep as much 'warmth' as possible within the food, but it is better to leave dry products such as cakes, breads and pastry uncovered. Place these on a piece of kitchen paper towel, to help absorb any moisture and prevent the base of the food getting soggy. These foods (like meat) should not be completely thawed in the microwave but given a standing time to complete the process.

Sauces, soups, casseroles, stews, fruits and vegetables thaw more quickly if you **break them up gently** with a fork during thawing. It is also helpful to choose a container which is large enough to contain boiling and bubbling up liquid on reheating, yet of such a shape that it will keep the thawed liquid close to the frozen block. Where foods contain pieces of ice which are not a part of a sauce, the ice can be removed as the microwave energy will simply be wasted on a part of the dish which is not required. Likewise, if thawing foods in which the liquid is simply water, remove any lumps of ice as they come free to speed the process.

Small, solid chunks of food such as chops or larger joints benefit from being **rearranged or turned** during thawing. If overheating occurs, use small pieces of foil secured by wooden cocktail sticks as a protection but, as always, ensure that the foil does not touch the cooking cavity walls or arcing will occur. Fish tails can be wrapped in foil for the same purpose.

Unless it is packed in foil, the food need not be removed from its freezer container, for the first 1 to 2 minutes of thawing time. It is then easier to transfer the food into the container to be used for cooking and serving, and continue with the remaining thawing and heating. If food *has* been packed in foil it can be held under cold running water to make it easier to remove the food.

Always make sure that cooked and frozen meat and poultry dishes are thoroughly heated through before serving. Unless otherwise stated, the weights given for thawing in the A–Z section are for the prepared food *before* freezing – another reason for making sure your freezer labelling is efficient!

Reheating food
Reheating food is fast and efficient and, when correctly reheated, food will not get that sad, unpalatable look that can occur when you use a conventional hob or oven. However, it is essential to ensure that foods are very hot, particularly meat, poultry and game, simply because many warm, half-heated foods can cause food poisoning.

Recently, we have been hearing a great deal about the possible link between the reheating of previously cooked, chilled or frozen food and the activation of bacteria which can cause food poisoning. Research has indicated that microwave cookers can vary in their ability to heat foods evenly; in fact, those of us who have been involved with microwave cooking from the beginning are well aware of the 'hot and cold spots' that may occur in the earliest cookers, and the steps and modifications taken by manufacturers to help towards eliminating these. (Much can be done by the cook, of course, by stirring, turning and rearranging foods during cooking and – if possible – reheating.)

Guidelines so far issued by the Ministry of Agriculture, Fisheries and Food advise that 'a minimum of 70°C should be achieved throughout the heated food' so that 'food-poisoning micro-organisms – if present' – should not survive. In other words, to ensure safety, **reheat food 'until piping hot right through'**. They also, in their statement underline 'the need for consumers to take care to follow normal kitchen hygiene practice. As with conventional forms of food heating, people should make sure that microwaved foods are thoroughly heated to make them safe . . . if, on the first heating, there is evidence that this has not been achieved, the food should be returned to the oven for a further heating period. If commonsense practices such as these are followed, the dangers from consuming undercooked foods will be avoided.'

Tips for reheating
When reheating slices of meat or poultry, always spoon over some gravy or stock. This will prevent the meat from heating too quickly and dehydrating. To avoid loss of moisture, cover most foods with a lid, plate or clear film. Prick this first to allow steam to escape.

As when thawing, 'dry' foods such as cooked bread rolls and pastries should not be covered as this causes the moisture drawn out by the action of the microwaves to condense and return to the food, making it soggy. Place such foods on a rack and/or a piece of kitchen paper towel. Always remove them from the microwave when warm to the touch, not hot, otherwise they will harden on cooling.

A meal on a plate will take about $3\frac{1}{2}$ to $4\frac{1}{2}$ minutes to reheat, but much depends on what is on the plate, so it is worth checking it from time to time during the reheating process. Should you want to reheat more than one 'plated' meal, stacking rings made of plastics can be used. However, the more food in the microwave cooker, the longer the reheating time. And one plateful invariably heats more slowly than another, so they need checking and re-arranging from time to time.

Correct arrangement of the food on the plate will help to achieve the best results; thought should be given to the density and texture of the food. Let's take slices of cooked meat, creamed potatoes and peas: potatoes are dense and take longer to heat than the meat or peas. So, rather than arranging them in a pile, flatten them out so that they are not so thick. The peas will heat quickly as they are small; these are best arranged in a pile. As the meat is thin it heats up quickly; cover it with gravy so that it will not overheat or dry out.

Chapter 3

An A to Z of Freezing and Thawing

The timings given in this section are based on a microwave cooker with a 700-watt output. See page 20 if you have a cooker with a lower output. For full explanations of the methods shown throughout this section in bold type (e.g. dry sugar, sugar syrup), turn to pages 12 and 13. Blanching refers to conventional blanching. Microwave thawing times for some fruits and vegetables are calculated on their weight before preparation, so weigh produce and label the freezer bags or boxes before proceeding.

A

APPLES

Cooking apples freeze better than dessert apples. (Freezing softens the texture of 'eating' apples, so they cannot be eaten like fresh ones.) Peel, core and slice them, discarding any bruised pieces. Have some lemon juice handy to prevent the slices from browning if the quantity is large. Cook, **purée** and freeze the purée, or use the **dry sugar** or **sugar syrup** method. If using dry sugar, blanch the slices first for 1 to 2 minutes in boiling water; drain, and cool.

Freezer storage   12 months

Purée   *To thaw*
Put into a small bowl; cover
Full power (100%)
For 225 g/8 oz, allow 2 minutes, breaking up with a fork after 1 and 2 minutes. Stand for 10 to 15 minutes, or until thawed.

Dry sugar   *To thaw and cook*
Put into a medium bowl; cover
Full power (100%)
For 450 g/1 lb, allow 8 to 10 minutes, breaking up with a fork once or twice during this time.

Sugar syrup   *To thaw*
Put into a medium bowl; cover
Full power (100%)
For 450 g/1 lb, allow 2 minutes, then gently break up with a fork and continue for a further 1 minute. Stand for 10 to 15 minutes, or until thawed. Do not cook these in the syrup or the fruit is likely to disintegrate. Just put the drained apples into a large bowl and cook, covered, for 8 minutes or until tender, stirring halfway through cooking.

APRICOTS

Choose firm, good-quality fruit. Either peel them or leave the skins on; remove and discard the stones as these can make the fruit bitter during storage. Halve or slice and pack in **sugar syrup**, or freeze as **purée**. Add 200 to 300 mg Vitamin C tablets to the syrup for every 450 g/1 lb pack to prevent discoloration.

Freezer storage   12 months

Halves or slices in sugar syrup
To thaw and cook
Put into a medium bowl and cover for thawing or use a large bowl, covered, for cooking.
Full power (100%)
For 450 g/1 lb allow 2 minutes, then gently separate with a fork. Continue for a further 2 minutes. Stand for 10 to 15 minutes until thawed. If cooking: allow 2 minutes, gently separate with a fork, then cook for 10 minutes or until syrup is boiling. Cook for a further 6 minutes or until apricots are cooked. Apricots tend to go mushy during cooking due to the large quantity of syrup so drain them after the first 4 minutes of thawing and return them to the medium bowl. Cook, covered, for 6 minutes or until tender. Otherwise, strain well when cooked.

Purée   *To thaw*
Use a small bowl; cover
Full power (100%)
For 225 g/8 oz, allow 2 minutes, breaking up with a fork after 1 and 2 minutes. Stand for 10 to 15 minutes or until thawed.

ARTICHOKES (GLOBE)

Choose first-class, fresh artichokes. Remove tough outer leaves and trim the rest by cutting across the tip of each leaf using scissors. Wash or soak thoroughly. Trim stalks and cut a cross in the base of each stem. **Blanch** in boiling water with 1 teaspoon of lemon juice added. Allow 5 minutes for small heads and 7 minutes for large ones. Cool, drain upside down and pack.

Freezer storage   12 months

To thaw and cook
Put into a shallow dish, upside down. Add 300 ml/½ pint water with 1 tablespoon lemon juice. Cover.
Full power (100%)
For 4, allow 25 minutes, turning over at the halfway stage. Stand, covered, for 10 minutes before serving.

ARTICHOKES (JERUSALEM)

Best frozen after cooking as a purée (if frozen whole, they tend to lose texture when cooked), but they can be **blanched** before freezing, then thawed and cooked.

For a purée Peel or scrub. Boil, drain and purée. Cool quickly and pack.

For slices Peel or scrub and slice thickly. Blanch in boiling water with 1 teaspoon of lemon juice for 5 minutes. Cool, drain and pack.

Freezer storage 3 months

Purée *To thaw and heat*
Put into a medium bowl; cover
Full power (100%)
For 450 g/1 lb, allow 5 minutes or until heated through. Break up with a fork after 3 minutes.
Sliced *To thaw and cook*
Use a medium bowl; cover
Full power (100%)
For 450 g/1 lb, allow 11 minutes or until tender, stirring halfway through. Stand, covered, for 5 minutes.

ASPARAGUS

Choose top-quality, very fresh asparagus, keep in a cool place while preparing it and freeze quickly. For short storage – one to two weeks – asparagus can be frozen unblanched, if thoroughly washed and drained first. For longer keeping, it must be **blanched**: Trim the stems; blanch thick ones for 4 minutes, medium for 3 minutes and thin ones for 2 minutes. Drain, dry and freeze loose in flat containers, head to tail as frozen asparagus can break easily. Interleave the layers. They can be **open-frozen** although there is a risk that the heads may break during packing.

Freezer storage
Unblanched: 2 weeks
Blanched: 12 months

To thaw and cook
Put into a shallow dish; cover
Full power (100%)
For 450 g/1 lb, allow 8 minutes or until tender. Separate as soon as possible, then arrange with the tips at the centre of the dish. If the asparagus has been open-frozen, arrange them with the tips at the centre of the dish before thawing and cooking.

AUBERGINES

Cut in half lengthways or peel and cut into 1- to 2.5-cm/$\frac{1}{2}$- to 1-inch slices. Add 2 tablespoons of lemon juice to the blanching water. Blanch for 5 minutes if halved, 3 minutes if sliced. Cool, drain and pack. If blanched in halves, they can later be used for stuffing but they will not be as stiff as unfrozen aubergine.

Freezer storage 12 months

Halved *To thaw*
Arrange on a plate; cover
Full power (100%)
For 2 large halves, allow 5 to 6 minutes
Sliced *To thaw and cook*
Use a medium bowl; cover
Full power (100%)
For 325 g/12 oz, allow 7 minutes. Halfway through, gently separate and rearrange the slices.

AVOCADO PEARS

Sliced or whole avocado is not suitable for freezing as it will turn black, but as a purée with the stone in the pack, this is less likely to happen.

The purée can be served cold, though the colour is not as attractive as a freshly prepared avocado. It is best to use the purée in recipes requiring cooked avocado. Remove the skin and stone. Purée the flesh with 1 teaspoon lemon juice for each avocado. If using for dessert, add sugar to taste. Return the whole stone to the purée; freeze.

Freezer storage 3 months

To thaw and cook
Use a very small bowl; cover
Full power (100%)
For 2 small fruits, allow $2\frac{1}{2}$ minutes. Break up the purée and remove the stone halfway through.

B

BACON, GAMMON and HAM

As salt tends to accelerate rancidity, the freezer storage life of bacon and ham is not as long as that of other meats. Any dish that includes bacon, gammon or ham should not be stored for more than 1 month. If left for too long in a freezer, the fat of bacon turns from white to pink and develops an 'off' taste. Foil sheets or containers are not suitable as the salt in the meat can cause pin-prick holes to appear in the wrapping, thus risking freezer burn. Vacuum packs can be left in the original packing, then overwrapped with heavy duty polythene for extra protection. Other bacon rashers, chops or gammon should be interleaved with either clear film or freezer-quality polythene to make subsequent separation easier. Overwrap and store flat. Wrap joints in heavy-duty polythene, expelling as much air as possible.

Freezer storage
Smoked joints: 2 months
Unsmoked joints: 1 month
Vacuum-packed smoked joints:
4 months
Vacuum-packed unsmoked joints:
1 month
Smoked rashers, chops, gammon steaks: 2 months
Unsmoked rashers, chops, gammon steaks: 2–3 weeks
Vacuum-packed, smoked rashers, chops, gammon steaks: 4 months
Vacuum-packed unsmoked rashers, chops, gammon steaks: 1 month

Bacon, Gammon and Ham Joints
To thaw
Stand meat on a trivet or upturned plate in a shallow dish; cover
Power settings 50% *and Defrost* (30%)
Allow 10 minutes on 50%, reduce to Defrost (30%) and allow 12 minutes per 450 g/1 lb. Turn over once during thawing. Wrap in foil and stand for 1 hour. Smaller cuts such as joints under 450 g/1 lb will thaw more quickly than large ones, so check during thawing to

ensure that they are not starting to cook. Stand for 30 minutes or until thawed. Meat should be completely thawed before cooking.

Rashers   *To thaw*
Place on a plate, cover with kitchen paper towel.
Power settings 50% *and Defrost* (30%)
Give 3 minutes on 50%. Remove any thawed rashers. For large quantities, reduce to Defrost (30%) and allow 10 minutes per 450 g/1 lb.

Gammon steaks   *To thaw*
Put on a shallow dish, cover with kitchen paper towel.
Full power (100%)
For 225 g/8 oz, allow 4 minutes. Rearrange halfway through thawing.

BANANAS
Not suitable for freezing as they turn black.

BATTERS
Pancakes Make batter and cook in the usual way. Cool, interleave each pancake with greaseproof paper and pack flat in a stack.

Freezer storage   3 months

Pancakes *To thaw*
Place on a plate
Full power (100%)
For 6 in a stack, allow 1½ to 2 minutes. Check frequently and remove thawed ones.

Yorkshire Pudding Make up batter and freeze, uncooked, in greased patty tins or small foil containers. Overwrap when frozen. They can then be cooked, uncovered, from frozen in a pre-heated hot oven at Gas 8, 450°F, 230°C for 25 minutes or until risen, brown and cooked.

BEANS
Broad, without pods Choose young, tender beans with no tough outer skins. Discard any starchy ones. Separate into small and large sizes. **Blanch:** Small for 2 minutes, large for 3 minutes. Cool,

30

drain and pack or open-freeze, pack.

Freezer storage 12 months

To thaw and cook
Put into a medium bowl; cover
Full power (100%)
For 450 g/1 lb, allow 11 minutes or
until cooked, stirring and gently break-
ing up after 3 and 9 minutes.

French Small ones can be kept
whole and the ends snipped off; large
ones are better sliced. **Blanch.** Small,
whole beans or sliced beans, allow 2
minutes; larger whole beans, allow 3
minutes. Cool, drain and pack or
open-freeze, then pack.

Runner Choose very fresh, top-
quality, straight beans; string them and
slice thickly. **Blanch** for 2 minutes.
Cool, drain and pack or open-freeze,
then pack.

Freezer storage 12 months

To thaw and cook
Use a large bowl; cover
Full power (100%)
For 450 g/1 lb, allow 14 minutes or
until tender, stirring halfway through.

BEEF
All beef products freeze well, except
for salted meat, as salt speeds up the
development of rancidity.

Brains Must be absolutely fresh.
Wash in salt water, snip off any pieces
of bone, all the fibres and any membrane. Drain well, pat dry, pack and
freeze.

Freezer storage 3 months

To thaw
Place on a plate; cover
Defrost (30%)
For 175 g/6 oz, allow 4 minutes, turning over after 2 and 3 minutes. Stand,
covered, for 5 to 10 minutes or until
thawed. Use at once.

Joints Wipe the meat over with a
clean cloth. Remove any extra fat and
pad any bones with wrapping. Wrap
well. Never stuff boneless joints first.

Freezer storage 12 months

To thaw
Stand meat on a trivet or upturned
plate set in a shallow dish; cover.
Power settings 50% *and Defrost* (30%)
For topside, boned and rolled sirloin
or forerib and pot-roast brisket, allow
10 minutes on 50%. Reduce power to
Defrost (30%), then allow 12 minutes
per 450 g/1 lb. Turn over once during
thawing. Wrap in foil and stand for 1
hour or until completely thawed. (*The
meat must be completely thawed before
cooking.*)

Kidneys These must be absolutely
fresh. Wash and remove cores and
membranes, trim off fat, then slice or
dice. Pack and freeze as soon as possible after purchase.

Freezer storage 3 months

To thaw
Put into a small bowl; cover
Full power (100%)
For 325 g/12 oz, allow 1 minute.
Gently separate with a fork, then cook
a further 30 seconds to 1 minute.
Stand, covered, for 10 to 15 minutes
or until thawed.

Mince Use freshly minced beef and
pack and freeze as soon as possible.
Make flat packages to save time at the
thawing stage.

Freezer storage 3 months

To thaw
Put into a large bowl; cover
Power settings 50% *and Defrost* (30%)
After 5 minutes on 50%, reduce power
to defrost (30%) and allow 12 minutes
per 450 g/1 lb, breaking up frequently
with a fork to speed up thawing.

Ox Heart Hearts must be absolutely
fresh. Wash and remove tubes, trim
off fat and slice, if necessary. Pack as
soon as possible after purchase.

Freezer storage 3 months

To thaw
Put into a shallow dish; cover
Full power (100%)

For sliced hearts weighing 325 g/12 oz, allow 2 minutes, then stand for 10 minutes or until thawed. For larger quantities and whole hearts, allow 3 minutes, then stand for 10 minutes or until thawed.

Ox Liver Liver must be absolutely fresh. Wash and trim, then slice and interleave. Over-wrap before packing, and pack and freeze as soon as possible.

Freezer storage 3 months

To thaw
Put into a shallow dish or medium bowl; cover
Full power (100%)
For 225 g/8 oz, allow 2 to 2½ minutes. Separate the pieces after 1 or 2 minutes. Stand, covered, for 8 minutes or until thawed.

Oxtail Trim off fat and gristle; cut into neat pieces for packing.

Freezer storage 6 months

To thaw
Put into a large bowl; cover
Full power (100%)
For 900 g/2 lb, allow 3½ minutes, separating and rearranging after 2 minutes. Stand, covered, for 15 minutes or until thawed.

Ox Tongue Tongue must be absolutely fresh and keeps longer if unsalted. (Most tongue is sold salted; unsalted tongue may be ordered from family butchers'.) Wipe the tongue with a clean cloth. Trim off any gristle. Wrap well.

Freezer storage 3 months; 1 month, if salted

To thaw
Place in a shallow dish; cover
Power settings 50% *and Defrost* (30%)
Allow 10 minutes on 50%. Reduce power to Defrost (30%) and allow 11 minutes per 450 g/1 lb, turning over once during thawing. Wrap in foil and stand for 1 hour or until thawed.

Sausages Avoid freezing in a block as sausages are difficult to separate

after freezing. Interleave before packing or open freeze, then pack.

Freezer storage 3 months

To thaw
Arrange the sausages evenly on a plate. Cover with a kitchen paper towel.
Full power (100%)
For 225 g/8 oz, allow 2½ minutes. Remove any sausages once almost thawed. Stand for 3 to 4 minutes before cooking, then cook conventionally. *Never fry in the microwave.*

Steaks and escalopes Prepare as for joints but, when packing the pieces of meat, interleave to allow for easier separation when frozen – or open freeze, then pack.

Freezer storage 12 months

To thaw
Place the pieces on a plate; cover
Power settings 50% *and Defrost* (30%)
Allow 5 minutes on 50%, then reduce power to Defrost (30%) and allow a further 10 minutes per 450 g/1 lb.

Sweetbreads These must be absolutely fresh. Wash well in salt water. Dry on kitchen paper towel; pack and freeze.

Freezer storage 3 months

To thaw
Put into a medium bowl; cover
Full power (100%)
For 225 g/8 oz, allow 1 minute. Separate and stand, covered, for 15 minutes or until thawed.

Stewed beef Trim off fat and gristle and cut into cubes. Pack.

Freezer storage 6 months

To thaw
Place in a medium bowl; cover
Full power (100%)
For 450 g/1 lb, allow 4 minutes, stirring halfway through. Stand, covered, for 5 to 10 minutes or until thawed.

Tripe Must be absolutely fresh. Wash well in salt water, then dry and cut into slices. Pack.

Freezer storage 3 months

To thaw
Put into a medium bowl; cover
Full power (100%) *and Defrost* (30%)
For 325 g/12 oz, allow 2 minutes on
Full power (100%). Turn over and
reduce power to Defrost (30%) for $4\frac{1}{2}$
minutes; separate and rearrange after 3
minutes. Stand for 5 to 10 minutes.

BEETROOT
Beetroot must be cooked before freezing. To freeze whole, pick very small,
young ones, about 2.5 cm/1 inch in
diameter. Cook, cool quickly and peel.
For large maincrop beets; cook, cool
quickly, peel and slice or dice. Pack.

Freezer storage 6 months

Small, whole beets *To thaw*
Put into a small bowl; cover
Full power (100%)
For 225 g/8 oz, allow $2\frac{1}{4}$ minutes, re-
arranging after $1\frac{1}{2}$ minutes. Stand for
10 to 15 minutes or until thawed.

Sliced or diced *To thaw*
Put into a shallow dish; cover
Full power (100%)
For 225 g/8 oz, allow $1\frac{3}{4}$ minutes. Gently
separate after 1 minute. Stand, covered,
for 10 minutes or until thawed.

BILBERRIES
Treat as for **Blackberries**

BISCUITS (Uncooked mixture)
Prepare the biscuit dough and freeze,
uncooked in a roll. When required,
partially thaw dough, cut roll in slices
and bake in the usual way. Alter-
natively, roll out the dough, cut into
desired shapes and **open-freeze**, then
interleave to prevent them sticking together.

Freezer storage 3 months

To thaw
Stand uncooked roll on a plate, un-
covered
Full power (100%)
For a 225 g/8 oz roll, give 30 seconds.
Check frequently to see the mixture

does not over-soften. Stand, covered,
for 5 minutes or until thawed.

Biscuit shapes are best left to thaw at
room temperature. Spread out on a
baking tray and leave for about 30
minutes.

BLACKBERRIES, BILBERRIES, LOGANBERRIES and RASPBERRIES
Choose firm, dry, clean, fully ripened,
top-quality berries. Discard any that
are not up to standard. If unsure how
clean the fruit is, then gently wash and
drain it. Whole dry fruit is suitable for
freezing directly in bags, or for **open-
freezing, dry sugar** pack and **sugar
syrup** methods. Over-ripe or wet fruit
should be **puréed**.

Freezer storage
Whole fruit: 12 months
Purée: 6 months

Open-frozen *To thaw*
Berries are more likely to hold their
shape if thawed at room temperature,
on kitchen paper towel. If possible,
serve before thawed to a pulp.
Dry sugar *To thaw*
Use a large bowl; cover
Full power (100%)
For 450 g/1 lb, allow $4\frac{1}{2}$ minutes.
Gently stir halfway through thawing.
Stand, covered, for 5 minutes.
Thaw and cook As above but allow 9
minutes and stir halfway through cook-
ing. Standing time is not required.
Sugar syrup *To thaw*
Use a medium bowl; cover
Full power (100%)
For 450 g/1 lb, allow 2 minutes. Gently
break up with a fork and continue for 1
minute more. Stand for 10 to 15 min-
utes or until thawed. Do not cook, as
there is far more syrup than necessary
and the fruit disintegrates.
Purée *To thaw*
Use a small bowl; cover
Full power (100%)
For 225 g/8 oz, allow 2 minutes, breaking up with a fork after 1 and 2
minutes. Stand for 10 to 15 minutes or
until thawed.

BLACK PUDDING
Black and white puddings must be absolutely fresh. Wash in salt water, dry and pack.

Freezer storage   3 months

To thaw
Place on a plate; cover
Full power (100%)
For a 450 g/1 lb piece, allow 1 minute. Cook and serve immediately.

BLACKCURRANTS and
RED AND WHITE CURRANTS
Can be frozen raw or puréed. Choose only firm, top-quality ripe currants and discard any green or wizened fruit. Suitable to freeze directly in bags, to **open-freeze**, to **dry sugar** pack, for the **sugar syrup** method or as purée. For storing fruit to make jam later on, **blanch** the currants for 1 minute before freezing to help retain the pectin quality.

Blackcurrant juice can be frozen in ice cube trays then removed, individually wrapped and stored for up to 6 months.

Freezer storage
Berries: 12 months
Pulp: 6 to 7 months

Open-frozen   *To thaw*
Use a shallow dish; cover
Defrost (30%)
For 225 g/8 oz, give 3 minutes. Gently rearrange after 1½ minutes. Stand for 10 minutes or until thawed.
Dry sugar   *To thaw*
Use a medium bowl; cover
Full power (100%)
For 450 g/1 lb, allow 3 minutes, gently stirring halfway through. Stand, covered, for 5 minutes.
Thaw and cook   as above allowing 8½ minutes – or until tender, stirring halfway through.
Sugar syrup   *To thaw*
Use a medium bowl; cover
Full power (100%)
For 450 g/1 lb, allow 2 minutes. Gently break up with a fork and continue for 1 minute more. Stand for 10 to 15 minutes or until thawed. Cooking is not recommended as there is far more syrup than would normally be used and the fruit disintegrates into the liquid. However, for cooking, drain the currants after thawing and place in a large bowl. Cook, covered, for 4½ minutes or until tender, stirring halfway through.
Purée   *To thaw*
Use a small bowl; cover
Full power (100%)
For 225 g/8 oz, allow 2 minutes, breaking up with a fork after 1 and 2 minutes. Stand for 10 to 15 minutes or until thawed.

Frozen juice   *To thaw*
Use a jug, uncovered
Full power (100%)
For 300 ml/½ pint, allow 2 minutes, breaking up with a fork halfway through. Stir before standing for 10 to 15 minutes – or until thawed.

BOYSENBERRIES
Treat as for **Blackberries**

BRANDY OR RUM BUTTER
Make sure the butter is fresh and if bought, that it is well within the 'sell by' date. Overwrap to prevent damage. If homemade, spoon into a small bowl, smooth top and cover.

Freezer storage   3 months

To thaw
If bought, remove from wrapping and stand on a plate, uncovered. If homemade, remove cover and leave butter in bowl.
Defrost (30%)
For 225 g/8 oz, allow 1 to 1½ minutes. Stand for 5 minutes, checking frequently to see it does not over-soften.

BREAD
Wrap well as whole loaves or in a convenient number of slices. Bread rolls and croissants can be individually wrapped, or in bags. Some crusty breads separate from their crust when

thawed; avoiding this is a matter of trial and error!

Freezer storage   4 to 6 weeks

To thaw
Wrap loaf in a clean cotton or linen towel, greaseproof paper or kitchen paper towel.
Full power (100%)
For a large loaf, allow $2\frac{1}{2}$ minutes. After thawing, leave to stand for 5 minutes. If necessary, return to the microwave for 2 more minutes.
For 1 slice or 1 bread roll, allow 30 seconds to 1 minute. Place on kitchen paper towel. Remove when warm to the touch. Leave to stand for a minute or two before using.

Bread dough (uncooked)
Extra yeast is recommended – about half as much again as given in the recipe. Freeze when dough is mixed but before rising or kneading. Place in an oiled polythene bag. (The dough can be frozen after rising and knocking back, but the cooked results are not as good). It is not suitable for thawing or cooking in a microwave, as the quick heat can kill the yeast. Instead, thaw bread dough for 5 to 6 hours at room temperature. Continue as the recipe directs.

Freezer storage   5 weeks

Part-baked rolls and bread
Keep in the original wrappers. Over-wrap for extra protection (the original wrapping may be porous). Not suitable for thawing and cooking in the micro-wave. Instead, thaw at room temperature and bake in a conventional oven, following manufacturer's instructions.

Breadcrumbs   Pack in suitable quantities for use.

Freezer storage   2 months

Use straight from the bag. No need to thaw.

BROCCOLI and CALABRESE
Choose compact heads. Remove leaves and trim stalks. Wash in salted water.

Blanch small heads for 3 minutes, medium ones for 4 minutes, large ones for 5 minutes. Cool and drain. Pack top to tail in shallow flat boxes to avoid damaging flower heads, or **open-freeze**, then pack.

Freezer storage   12 months

To thaw and cook
Use a shallow dish; cover
Full power (100%)
For 225 g/8 oz, allow 6 minutes. Gently separate and rearrange, with the florets towards the centre of the dish. Continue cooking for a further 6 minutes or until tender. If open-frozen, arrange with the florets to the centre before starting thawing.

BRUSSELS SPROUTS
Choose very fresh, small, tight, un-damaged sprouts. Prepare as usual, dividing them into small and medium sizes. **Blanch** small ones 3 minutes, medium ones 4 minutes. Cool, drain and pack or **open-freeze**, then pack.

Freezer storage   12 months

To thaw and cook
Put into a large bowl with 2 table-spoons water; cover
Full power (100%)
For 225 g/8 oz, allow 9 minutes, stir-ring halfway through. Stand, covered, for 3 minutes.

BUTTER
Make sure it is fresh and well within the 'sell by' date. Over-wrap to prevent damage.

Freezer storage
Savoury butter: 2 months
Salted butter: 3 months
Unsalted butter: 6 months
If kept for longer the butter may develop a granular texture.

To thaw
Remove wrapping, stand on a plate, un-covered.
Defrost (30%)
For 225 g/8 oz, allow 1 to $1\frac{1}{2}$ minutes. Stand for 5 minutes. Check frequently to ensure it does not over-soften.

C

CABBAGE
All frozen cabbage must subsequently be cooked, as it will not be suitable for salads. Red, Spring cabbage and White cabbage: Use only very good, standard, fresh produce. Wash thoroughly, finely shred. For white cabbage, add one tablespoon of vinegar to blanching water to improve colour. **Blanch** all cabbage for 1 minute. Cool, drain and pack.

Freezer storage   12 months

To thaw and cook
Use a large bowl; cover
Full power (100%)
For 450 g/1 lb white or red cabbage, allow 12 minutes or until cabbage is tender, stirring after 4 and 8 minutes.
For 450 g/1 lb spring cabbage, allow 10 minutes or until it is tender, stirring after 4 and 8 minutes.

CAKES
With fillings   Those with butter or whipped double cream filling or decoration may be frozen, but jam or other liquid fillings should be added after thawing. **Open-freeze** and pack in rigid containers.

Freezer storage   The time depends on the fillings.
Cream-filled: 2 months
Buttercream-filled: 3 months

To thaw
Stand on a plate.
Full power (100%)
For 1 small cake, allow about 1 minute. Leave to stand, covered, for 20 to 30 minutes before serving Slice cream-filled cakes while still part-frozen.

Undecorated cakes   Chocolate and some spices may slightly change their flavour during freezing. **Open-freeze** and pack for freezing. Do not sandwich with jam; simply place greaseproof paper between cakes and fill when thawed.

Freezer storage   6 months
To thaw
Place on a piece of kitchen paper towel on a plate; uncovered
Full power (100%)
For a 15- to 18-cm/6- to 7-inch cake, allow 1 minute; stand for 20 to 30 minutes or until thawed.

Swiss rolls   should be rolled up and frozen with lightly oiled and sugared greaseproof paper inside, then unrolled gently and filled after thawing.

Freezer storage   6 months

To thaw
Place on a piece of kitchen paper towel on a plate; cover
Full power (100%)
Allow 1 minute, checking after 30 seconds to make sure it has not thawed. Cover and leave to stand for 20 to 30 minutes, then gently unroll, fill and re-roll to serve.

Fruit cakes   Very rich fruit cakes such as Christmas cakes, can be stored in airtight tins for many months. Rich fruit cakes also store well in airtight tins. They can be frozen but not if topped with marzipan or icing. Leave to cool completely before wrapping.

Freezer storage   12 months

To thaw
Place on a piece of kitchen paper towel on a plate, uncovered
Full power (100%)
For a 20-cm/8-inch rich fruit cake, allow 2 minutes. Stand for 30 minutes to 1 hour, or until thawed.
For a light fruit cake, allow 1 minute; stand for 30 minutes or until thawed.

Soft-iced cakes   Open-freeze; wrap in freezer polythene and store in a rigid container.

Freezer storage   3 months

Not suitable for microwave thawing because of the water content of the icing and the speed at which it would thaw. Thaw at room temperature, removing wrapping before thawing to prevent it sticking to the icing. (The surface of the icing will go moist at first, but it dries out naturally when cake thaws completely.)

CALABRESE
Treat as for **Broccoli**

CARROTS
Do not freeze old, woody carrots. Larger, older ones should be sliced, diced etc. first. Young, tender carrots freeze well whole. Peel or scrub maincrop carrots, scrape or scrub new ones. **Blanch** for 3 minutes. Cool, drain and pack or **open-freeze**, then pack.

Freezer storage   12 months

Whole baby carrots   *To thaw and cook*
Use a medium bowl; cover
Full power (100%)
For 225 g/8 oz, allow 8 minutes or until tender, stirring halfway through.
Sliced or diced   *To thaw and cook*
Use a medium bowl; cover
Full power (100%)
For 225 g/8 oz, allow 7 minutes or until tender, stirring halfway through.

CAULIFLOWER
Use white, firm, solid-headed cauliflowers; trim and wash them thoroughly. Break or cut into florets. Add one tablespoon lemon juice to the blanching water to retain colour. **Blanch** for 3 minutes. Cool, drain and pack or **open-freeze** and then pack.

Freezer storage   6 months

To thaw and cook
Use a large bowl; cover
Full power (100%)
For 225 g/8 oz, allow 8 minutes or until tender, stirring halfway through.

CELERIAC
Do not use old woody celeriac. Slice first, then peel as it is easier. Dice if desired. **Blanch** for 4 minutes: treated in this way, celeriac can be kept separate or included in a mixture of root

vegetables for use in stews etc. Cool, drain and pack.

Freezer storage   12 months

Slice and diced   *To thaw and cook*
Use a medium bowl; cover
Full power (100%)
For 450 g/1 lb, allow 12 minutes or until tender, stirring halfway through.

CELERY
Frozen celery is only suitable for cooking as it loses crispness during thawing. Wash well, scrub if necessary and remove any stringy parts. Cut into 2.5-cm/1-inch pieces; **blanch** for 2 minutes. Cool, drain and pack.

Freezer storage   12 months

To thaw and cook
Use a medium bowl; cover
Full power (100%)
For 450 g/1 lb, allow 14 minutes or until tender, stirring halfway through.

CHEESE
Cheese spreads, curd, cottage and low fat cheeses are not suitable for freezing as they tend to go rubbery when thawed. Hard and soft cheeses such as Cheddar, Edam, full-fat cream cheese, Brie and blue cheeses are suitable, but hard cheeses tend to crumble when thawed. Cut large pieces of cheese into useful sizes, or grate it for cooking. Wrap in foil or clear film and over-wrap.

Freezer storage
Full-fat soft cheeses: 1 month
Soft cheeses: 3 months
Hard cheeses: 4 months

To thaw
Stand cheese on a plate; cover
Defrost (30%)
Hard cheese for 125 g/4 oz, allow 1 to 2 minutes.
Grated cheese for 225 g/8 oz, allow 2 minutes.
Full or medium-fat soft cheese for 75 g/3 oz, allow 1 to 2 minutes.
Blue cheese for 125 g/4 oz, give 1 to 2 minutes. Stand, covered, for 10 to 15 minutes.

CHERRIES

Although all cherries can be frozen, the white ones do not freeze well as they tend to discolour. Red and black varieties are recommended, as are the bitter-sweet types and Morellos. Cooked, sweetened cherries freeze well but should be used within 8 months.

Select only firm, good quality cherries. Remove the stalks and stone the fruit to prevent any subsequent 'off' flavours. Both **dry sugar** pack and **sugar syrup** methods are suitable, but choose the latter for long keeping. When making syrup for very sour cherries, add extra sugar and a few drops of ascorbic acid or lemon juice to prevent discoloration.

Freezer storage 12 months (if poached in syrup, 8 months)

Dry sugar *To thaw*
Place in a medium bowl; cover
Full power (100%)
For 450 g/1 lb, allow 3 minutes. Leave to stand, covered, for 5 minutes or until thawed. If cooking, allow 9 minutes, gently breaking up and stirring halfway through. No standing time is needed.

Sugar syrup *To thaw*
Place in a medium bowl; cover
Full power (100%)
For 450 g/1 lb, allow 2 minutes. Gently break up with a fork and continue for 1 minute more. Stand for 10 to 15 minutes or until thawed. Cooking is not recommended as much more syrup is used for freezing and the fruit disintegrates into the liquid. If cooked cherries are required, drain them after thawing and place in a large bowl. Cook, covered, for 5 minutes or until tender, stirring halfway through.

Cooked (poached) *To thaw*
Use a medium bowl; cover
Full power (100%)
For 450 g/1 lb, allow 3 minutes. Leave to stand, covered, for 5 minutes or until thawed. Stir.

CHICKEN and DUCK

Roasting and boiling fowls and capon-style birds
Ready-frozen birds should be transferred from shop to freezer as quickly as possible to avoid thawing. *Thawed chicken should not be re-frozen without cooking first.* Giblets should not be left inside the bird if it is to be freezer-stored for more than three months as they have a much shorter storage life than the bird itself. If possible, cook and freeze them separately, as stock.

Whole birds should not be stuffed before freezing; stuffing can develop an unpleasant flavour after a few months. There is also a risk that the stuffing may not be thoroughly heated through during cooking and thus may constitute a health hazard. Pack and over-wrap before freezing. For whole fresh chickens, pluck, draw and prepare the bird. Wipe with a clean cloth; truss, cover any protruding bones with foil or double-thickness greaseproof paper, then pack and over-wrap.

Freezer storage 12 months

Chicken joints and pieces Wipe with a clean cloth; pad any protruding bone ends with extra padding. Wrap individually, interleaving fillets with greaseproof paper before wrapping. Over-wrap for extra protection.

Freezer storage
Chicken: 12 months
Duck: 6 months

Whole or portions *To thaw*
Stand on a shallow dish or plate. Shield thin parts with strips of foil for extra protection.
Power setting 50%
Allow 7 minutes per 450 g/1 lb. Remove the giblets as soon as possible. Turn over halfway through thawing. Wrap tightly in foil and leave to stand for 20 to 30 minutes before cooking. (Portions do not need to be wrapped in foil.)

Do not cook poultry until fully thawed or there could be a health hazard.

Giblets Wash in salt water, rinse in fresh water, pat dry and pack separately from bird.

Freezer storage 3 months

To thaw
Place in a medium bowl; cover
Full power (100%)
Allow 2 minutes; separate and stand for 10 to 15 minutes or until thawed.

Livers Must be absolutely fresh. Can be separated from giblets before freezing. Individually wrapped, they can be stored in a bag until you have enough for pâté, or other recipes.

Freezer storage 3 months

To thaw
Put into a small bowl; cover
Full power (100%)
For 325 g/12 oz, allow 1 minute. Gently separate with a fork. Allow a further 30 seconds. Stand, covered, for 10 to 15 minutes or until thawed.

CHICORY
Not recommended for freezing as the texture changes.

CHINESE LEAVES
Not recommended for freezing as they go limp.

CHIPS
See **Potatoes**

CHOPS
See **Lamb, Pork** and **Veal**

CORN ON THE COB and CORN KERNELS
See **Sweetcorn**

COURGETTES (Zuccini)
Always use young, very fresh, small vegetables. Wipe; do not peel. Trim. Freeze whole, halved lengthwise or in thickish slices. **Blanch** whole courgettes for 2 to 3 minutes, depending on size; halved $1\frac{1}{2}$ minutes, sliced 1 minute. Cool, drain and pack. Can also be frozen cut into 1-cm/$\frac{1}{2}$-inch slices

and gently cooked in butter until just tender. Cool, drain and pack.

Freezer storage
Blanched: 12 months
Cooked in butter: 6 months

Blanched or cooked in butter
To thaw and cook/reheat
Use a large bowl; cover
Full power (100%)
For 450 g/1 lb, allow $10\frac{1}{2}$ minutes, stirring halfway through.

CRAB and LOBSTER
Only freeze cooked crab. Wipe dry. (If freshly cooked, let whole crab cool.) Wrap well. *Or* remove and discard inedible parts; pack the meat.

Freezer storage 1 month

Dressed or whole crab *To thaw*
Stand on a plate or shallow dish; cover
Full power (100%)
For 1 small crab, allow 1 minute. Leave to stand for 20 to 25 minutes or until thawed.

Crab or lobster meat *To thaw*
Stand on a plate; cover
Full power (100%)
For 400 g/14 oz, allow 2 minutes, turning the meat over halfway through. Break up the meat with a fork, removing any thawed pieces and microwave the remaining frozen pieces. Leave to stand for 10 minutes before serving.

CREAM
Single, soured and synthetic creams are not suitable for freezing.
Clotted cream may not always retain its texture so it is best to experiment with your favourite brand.

Double or whipping cream
Lightly whip with 1 tablespoon milk to 150 ml/$\frac{1}{4}$ pint cream. Pack in a plastic container, allowing headspace for expansion. If wished, whip cream and pipe into rosettes, then **open-freeze**. Pack in boxes, separating each rosette with a small piece of crumpled paper.

Freezer storage
Double/whipping cream: 2 months
Clotted cream: 1 month

To thaw
All cream is best thawed slowly in the refrigerator; in an emergency, remove the lid and thaw in the carton or container.
Defrost (30%)
Double cream, for 150 ml/¼ pint, allow 2½ minutes.
Whipping cream, for 150 ml/¼ pint, allow 2 minutes.
Break up and stir several times as it thaws, checking frequently to see that it is not heating. Stand, uncovered, for 10 to 15 minutes.

Rosettes: Place, still frozen on cake and allow to thaw at room temperature for about 20 minutes, or in the refrigerator for about 30 minutes.

CRUMPETS
Interleave with greaseproof paper, foil or clear film before packing or they will stick together. Thawing is not necessary as crumpets can be toasted from the frozen state.

Freezer storage 1 month

CUCUMBER
Cucumbers do not freeze well because of their high water content. They can be frozen in made-up dishes, especially in soups (see page 64).

D

DAMSONS
Select firm, good quality fruit, discarding any which is blemished. Damson skins may toughen in freezing and this is more apparent when they are then cooked by microwave. If not stoned, they can develop an almond flavour if kept for longer than 9 months. Pick them over, removing stems and leaves; wash, pat dry between tea towels on trays. Pack into strong big bags to have a free flow supply. You can also use the **sugar syrup** method, or they can be cooked and **puréed**.

Freezer storage
Without stones: 12 months
With stones: 3 months
Puréed: 12 months
Free flow unstoned: 9 months

Sugar syrup   *To thaw*
Use a medium bowl; cover
Full power (100%)
For 450 g/1 lb, allow 2 minutes. Gently break up with a fork and continue for 1 minute more. Stand, covered, for 10 to 15 minutes or until thawed. Cooking is not recommended as there is far more syrup than would normally be used and the fruit disintegrates into the liquid. However, they can be drained after thawing and transferred into a large bowl. Cook, covered, for 5 minutes or until tender, stirring halfway through.
Purée   *To thaw*
Use a small bowl, cover
Full power (100%)
For 225 g/8 oz, allow 2 minutes, breaking up with a fork after 1 and 2 minutes. Stand, covered, for 10 to 15 minutes or until thawed.
Free flow   *To thaw and cook*
To avoid tough skins, do not microwave: put frozen damsons into a saucepan with sugar to taste and a little water and stew gently on a conventional hob.

DRIPPING
Pack in storage containers.

Freezer storage   3 months

To thaw
Use a small bowl, uncovered
Defrost (30%)
For 225 g/8 oz, allow 1 to 1½ minutes. Stand for 5 minutes. Check frequently to ensure it does not over-soften.

DUCK
Treat as for **Chicken**.

Freezer storage   6 months

E

EGGS

Hard-boiled eggs, scrambled, or eggs in shells are not suitable for freezing. Hard-boiled and scrambled eggs turn rubbery; eggshells break. Egg yolks can be frozen but tend to thicken during the freezing process.

Whole eggs and egg yolks Break and lightly beat with either a pinch of salt or sugar to each egg – depending on whether they are to be used for a savoury or sweet dish. This helps prevent them thickening. Use plastic boxes with lids, leaving a headspace to allow for expansion. (Remember to label clearly whether salted or sugared!)

Egg whites No need to add sugar or salt; simply lightly beat.

Freezer storage 6 months

Eggs *To thaw*
Use a very small bowl; cover
Full power (100%)
For **two lightly beaten whole eggs,** allow 1 minute. Break up with a fork halfway through. Stand, covered, for 5 minutes.
For **two yolks,** allow 30 seconds. Stir with a fork. Stand, covered, for 10 minutes.
For **two whites,** allow 45 seconds. Place in a very small bowl, covered. Break up with a fork halfway through. Stand, covered, for 5 minutes.

ENDIVE

Unsuitable for freezing as it goes limp and discolours.

F

FENNEL

Remove any tough outer leaves and the hard base; cut into quarters. **Blanch** for 3 minutes. Drain, cool and pack.

Freezer storage 6 months
To thaw and cook
Use a medium bowl; cover
Full power (100%)
For 450 g/1 lb, allow 10 minutes or until tender. Separate and rearrange halfway through.

FIGS

Peel; leave whole, then use the **sugar syrup** method.

Freezer storage 3 months

To thaw
Use a small bowl, cover
Full power (100%)
For 450 g/1 lb figs, allow 3 minutes. Stand, covered, for 15 minutes or until thawed. Stir.

FISH

Also see **Crab** and **Lobster, Prawns, Scallops** and **Shrimps**
Freeze only freshest fish, on the day it is caught if possible. Scale, gut, wash and dry.

Fresh fish portions Scale and gut. Cut into steaks or fillets, if necessary. Wash in salt water. Dry. Wrap steaks separately and interleave fillets before wrapping.

Freezer storage 6 months
To thaw and cook
Place in a shallow dish; arrange steaks with thin ends to the centre; cover
Full power (100%)
For 225 g/8 oz fillets, allow 5 minutes; steaks, including salmon, 6 minutes. Gently separate fillets or pieces halfway through. Stand, covered, for 3 to 4 minutes to finish cooking.

Smoked fish and fillets (e.g. kipper) Wrap individually, then overwrap. For smoked salmon, interleave the slices first to prevent them sticking together.

Freezer storage 2 months

To thaw
Place on a plate; cover

Defrost (30%)
For 125 to 150 g/4 to 5 oz, allow 1 to
1½ minutes. Stand, covered, for 5 to 10
minutes or until thawed.

Smoked salmon   *To thaw*
Place on a plate, uncovered
Full power (100%)
For 200 g/7 oz, allow 30 seconds, turning over after 15 seconds. Gently separate the salmon from the interleaving
and spread out over the plate. Leave to
stand, covered, for 25 to 30 minutes or
until thawed.

Roes   Herring and cod roes must be
absolutely fresh. Wash, rinse, dry and
pack. Smoked cod's roe: Wipe with a
clean cloth and pack.

Freezer storage   1 month

To thaw
Place on a plate; cover
Defrost (30%)
For 225 g/8 oz smoked roes, allow 2 to
3 minutes; for fresh roes, 1 to 2
minutes. Stand, covered, for 5 to 10
minutes or until thawed.

Whole fish   An 'ice-glazing' process
gives best results as this forms a coating and prevents evaporation. Place the
fish on a wire tray and **open-freeze**
until firm. Have ready a bowl of ice-
cold water. Pull each fish through
the water several times, resting it on a
wire tray in the freezer for 30 minutes
between immersions, until it is completely coated with a thin film of ice.
Wrap each fish, then over-wrap.

Whole salmon   Can be stuffed with
paper to retain the shape. Wrap and
over-wrap for protection.

Freezer storage
Oily fish (e.g. herrings): 1 month
Salmon and trout: 1 month
White fish (e.g. plaice): 6 months

Oily fish (herrings, mackerel)
To thaw and cook
Place in a shallow dish; cover
Full power (100%)
For 2, allow 6 minutes. Stand, covered,
for 3 minutes before serving to finish
off the cooking.

Whole salmon   *To thaw and cook*
Place on a large plate and shield thin
ends with foil; cover
Power settings 50% and Full (100%)
For 900 g/2 lb salmon, allow 9 minutes
on 50%; stand for 25 minutes. Microwave for a further 5 minutes and stand,
covered, for 30 minutes or until
thawed. (Remove any paper stuffing.)
To cook, increase power to Full
(100%). Cook, covered, for 8 to 10
minutes or until the flesh is opaque.

Trout   *To thaw and cook*
Place on a large round or oval plate;
shield thin ends with small pieces of
foil; cover
Full power (100%)
For 2 medium trout (275 g/10 oz each)
give 8 minutes, turning over after 3
minutes. If desired, brush with a little
butter and continue cooking. Leave to
stand for 3 minutes before serving.

White fish (whole plaice or sole)
To thaw and cook
Place on a large plate; shield thin ends
with foil; cover
Power settings 50% and Full (100%)
For 450 g/1 lb, allow 5 to 6 minutes on
50%. Stand, covered, for 4 minutes.
Increase power to Full (100%). Cook,
covered, for 4 minutes or until flesh is
opaque.

G

GAMMON
See **Bacon**

GOOSE
Old fatty birds should be used within
2 months of freezing. Prepare as for
Chicken.

Freezer storage   6 months

To thaw
Place in a shallow container, standing
on an upturned plate or trivet. Shield
thin parts with small pieces of foil and
cover bird with kitchen paper towel.
Power setting 50%
Allow 6 to 7 minutes per 450 g/1 lb.

Remove the giblets as soon as possible. Turn over 3 times during thawing. Immerse in cold water for 30 minutes after thawing to ensure the bird is completely thawed. Remove, drain and dry. *Cook in a conventional oven only when completely thawed.*

Giblets   Wash in salt water, rinse in fresh water, pat dry and pack.

Freezer storage   3 months

To thaw
Place in a medium bowl; cover
Full power (100%)
Allow 2 minutes. Separate and stand for 10 to 15 minutes or until thawed.

GOOSEBERRIES

Fully-ripe dessert fruit does not give particularly good results when frozen because it tends to go mush and is suitable only for pies and tarts. It is best to use the fully grown but still hard, only-just-ripe or even slightly immature berries for freezing whole. Wash only if necessary and pat dry between tea towels laid on a tray, then pack into bags for a free-flow supply. When frozen the 'tops and tails' rub away easily from the fruit, though this is rather a painful process, so unless just a few berries are needed, it is better to 'top and tail' before freezing – in the usual way. Suitable, too, for **dry sugar** pack, **sugar syrup** or **purée** methods.

Freezer storage   12 months

Dry sugar   *To thaw and cook*
Place in a large bowl; cover
Full power (100%)
For 450 g/1 lb, allow 10 minutes, breaking up and stirring halfway through.
Sugar syrup   *To thaw*
Place in a medium bowl; cover
Full power (100%)
For 450 g/1 lb, allow 2 minutes. Gently break up with a fork and continue for 1 minute more. Stand for 10 to 15 minutes or until thawed. Cooking is not recommended as there is far more syrup than would normally be used and the fruit disintegrates into the liquid.

However, for cooking, drain the gooseberries after thawing and place in a large bowl. Cook, covered, for 5 minutes or until tender, stirring halfway through.

Purée   *To thaw*
Use a small bowl; cover
Full power (100%)
For 225 g/8 oz, allow 2 minutes, breaking up with a fork after 1 and 2 minutes. Stand, covered, for 10 to 15 minutes or until thawed.
Open-frozen   *To thaw and cook*
Use a large bowl; cover
Full power (100%)
For 450 g/1 lb, allow 9 minutes, breaking up and stirring halfway through, and adding sugar to taste.

GRAPEFRUIT and Ugli fruit
Not suitable for freezing whole.
Segments   Remove the peel and separate fruit into segments. Use the **dry sugar** method.
Juice   Squeeze grapefruit; remove pips. Pour juice into suitable containers, leaving headspace for expansion.

Freezer storage   12 months

Segments   *To thaw*
Place in a small bowl; cover
Full power (100%)
For 450 g/1 lb grapefruit (weight before peeling), allow 2 minutes, breaking up and stirring halfway through.

Juice   *To thaw*
Use a jug, uncovered
Full power (100%)
For 300 ml/½ pint, allow 2 minutes, breaking up with a fork halfway through. Stir before standing for 10 to 15 minutes or until thawed.

GRAPES
Grapes stay quite firm after freezing in this way; they are suitable for fresh fruit salads. Discard any damaged fruit; wash, dry; skin and remove pips if desired. Use the **sugar syrup** method.

Freezer storage   12 months

To thaw
Use a medium bowl; cover
Full power (100%)
For 450 g/1 lb, allow 4 minutes, gently separating halfway through. Stand, covered, 15 minutes or until thawed.

GREENGAGES
Treat as for **Damsons**

H

HAM
See **Bacon**

HARE
Joints   Treat as for **Chicken**
For a whole fresh hare, hang for the required time (7 to 10 days), then skin and prepare for the chosen cooking method. Draw and wipe inside and out with a clean, damp cloth. Cut into joints, if required. Wrap up, with extra protection around sharp, bony places and over-wrap to keep any odour from pervading the freezer.

Freezer storage   6 months

Joints and pieces   *To thaw*
Stand on a shallow dish or plate. Shield thin parts with strips of foil for extra protection.
Power setting 50%
Allow 7 minutes per 450 g/1 lb. Turn over halfway through thawing. Wrap tightly in foil and leave to stand for 20 to 30 minutes before cooking. (Portions do not need to be wrapped in foil.) Do not cook until fully thawed.

Whole hare   *To thaw*
Treat as joints, above.

HEARTS
See **Beef, Lamb** and **Pork**

44

I

ICE CREAM and SORBETS
Homemade   Freeze in polythene boxes. If to be used soon, freeze in the serving dish making sure the dish is freezer proof and not fragile. It must be securely covered.

Bought   Store as quickly as possible after purchase; do not re-freeze if thawed. Most suppliers pack ice cream in packets or containers suitable for the freezer.

Freezer storage
Homemade: 3 months
Bought: 1 month

Microwave tip
For ices and sorbets (except bought 'soft-scoop' iceam cream), microwave on Full power (100%) for 10 to 20 seconds to soften slightly and make them easier to serve.

K

KALE
Choose top-quality, very fresh kale. Remove leaves from stems, wash well. **Blanch** for 3 minutes. Cool, drain and pack.

Freezer storage   12 months

To thaw and cook
Treat as for **Cabbage**

KIDNEYS
See **Beef, Lamb, Pork** and **Veal**

KIWI FRUIT
The firm texture is lost during freezing but the fruit can be added to a fruit salad. Remove skin. Slice fruit and use the **dry sugar** method.

Freezer storage   12 months

Dry sugar   *To thaw*
Place in a shallow dish; cover

Full power (100%)
For 4 fruits, about 450 g/1 lb total weight, allow 2½ minutes. Gently separate with a knife and rearrange after 2 minutes. Stand, covered, for 10 minutes or until thawed.

KOHL-RABI
Do not freeze any kohl-rabi bigger than a small orange. If possible, use very small ones not much larger than 2.5 cm/1 inch in diameter; peel thinly and freeze whole after blanching. Larger ones should be peeled thinly and diced. **Blanch** for 3 minutes if whole and for 2 minutes, if diced. Drain, cool and pack. Older kohl-rabi can be cooked, mashed and then frozen.

Freezer storage   12 months

To thaw and cook
Treat as for **Turnip**

Mashed   *To thaw and heat*
Use a medium bowl; cover
Full power (100%)
For 450 g/1 lb, allow 5 minutes or until heated through, breaking up with a fork after 3 minutes.

L

LAMB
All lamb is suitable for freezing.

Brains   Must be absolutely fresh. Wash in salt water, snip off any pieces of bone, skin and fibre. Dry and pack.

Freezer storage   3 months

To thaw
Use a medium bowl; cover
Defrost (30%)
For 175 g/6 oz, allow 4 minutes, turning over after 2 and 3 minutes. Stand, covered, for 5 to 10 minutes or until thawed. Use at once.

Chops and cutlets   Treat as for joints (below). Interleave with greaseproof paper to allow for easier separation after freezing. Or, **open-freeze**, and then pack in large strong bags.

Freezer storage   9 months

To thaw
Arrange on a plate or shallow dish with the thin part of the chops facing the centre. Cover with kitchen paper towel.
Power settings 50% and Defrost (30%)
Allow 4 minutes on 50%. Reduce power to Defrost (30%) and allow 10 minutes per 450 g/1 lb. Separate if necessary halfway through; sooner, if only one or two chops are being thawed. As chops vary in thickness, check frequently and remove any thawed ones as soon as possible.

Hearts   Must be absolutely fresh. Wash and remove tubes, trim off fat. Pack and freeze as soon as possible.

Freezer storage   3 months

To thaw
Use a shallow dish; cover
Full power (100%)
For 2 lambs hearts, 325 g/12 oz total weight, allow 2 minutes. Stand, covered, for 10 minutes or until thawed.

Joints   Wipe the meat with a clean cloth and remove any extra fat. Pad any bones with extra wrapping; wrap well. Never stuff boneless joints before freezing. Over-wrap.

Freezer storage   9 months

To thaw
Stand meat on a trivet or upturned plate in a shallow dish. Shield thin ends (e.g. of legs) with small pieces of foil.
Power settings 50% and Defrost (30%)
For legs, rolled breast and boned, rolled shoulder, allow 10 minutes on 50%. Reduce power to Defrost (30%) and allow 12 minutes per 450 g/1 lb, turning over once during thawing. Wrap in foil and stand for 1 hour.
For crown roasts or neck of lamb, treat as above but stand, covered, for 30 minutes. All meat must be completely thawed before cooking.

Kidneys   Must be absolutely fresh.

Wash and remove cores, trim off fat. Pack and freeze as soon as possible.

Freezer storage 3 months

To thaw
Use a small bowl; cover
Full power (100%)
For 325 g/12 oz, allow 1 minute. Gently separate with a fork, then allow a further 30 seconds. Stand, covered, for 10 to 15 minutes or until thawed.

Liver Must be absolutely fresh. Wash and trim, or wash, trim, slice and interleave. Pack and freeze as soon as possible.

Freezer storage 3 months

To thaw
Use a small dish or small bowl; cover
Full power (100%)
For 225 g/8 oz, allow 2 to 2½ minutes, separating after 1 or 2 minutes. Stand, covered, for 8 minutes or until thawed.

Mince Use freshly minced lamb, and freeze as soon as possible. Make flat packages in convenient portions to save time when thawing.

Freezer storage 3 months

To thaw
Use a large bowl; cover
Power settings 50% *and Defrost* (30%)
Allow 5 minutes on 50%. Reduce power to Defrost (30%) and allow 12 minutes per 450 g/1 lb, breaking up frequently with a fork to speed up the thawing.

Stewing lamb Trim off fat and gristle, cut into cubes or neat pieces. Pack.

Freezer storage 6 months

To thaw
Use a medium bowl; cover
Full power (100%)
For 450 g/1 lb, allow 4 minutes, stirring halfway through thawing. Stand, covered, for 5 to 10 minutes or until thawed.

Sweetbreads Must be absolutely fresh. Wash in salt water. Pat dry; pack.

Freezer storage 3 months

To thaw
Use a medium bowl; cover
Full power (100%)
For 225 g/8 oz, allow 1 minute. Separate and stand, covered, for 15 minutes or until thawed.

Tongue Must be absolutely fresh and keeps longer if unsalted. Wipe with a clean cloth; trim and wrap well.

Freezer storage
Unsalted: 3 months
Salted: 1 month

To thaw
Use a medium bowl; cover
Full power (100%)
For 400 g/14 oz, allow 2 minutes. Separate, then stand, covered, for 15 minutes or until thawed.

LARD
Treat as for **Butter**

Freezer storage 3 months

LEEKS
Choose young, fresh, slender leeks of even size. Trim off most of the green leaves. Halve lengthwise and wash well to remove all the grit. **Blanch** 1 minute. Cool, drain and pack. To avoid any odour permeating through the packaging, use plastic boxes.

Freezer storage 12 months

To thaw and cook
Use a medium bowl; cover
Full power (100%)
For 450 g/1 lb, allow 10 minutes or until tender, breaking up and stirring halfway through.

LEMONS and LIMES
As the skins soften, whole fruit is only suitable for making into slices for drinks or kitchen purposes. Wash, dry, wrap fruit individually, then pack.

Slices and grated rind Wash and dry fruit before slicing and/or grating. **Open-freeze** and pack.

Juice Squeeze fruit, remove pips. Freeze juice in small quantities: Ice cube trays are useful. Once frozen, transfer cubes to plastic bags.

Freezer storage   12 months

To thaw
Place whole fruit on a plate, uncovered; slices or grated rind in a very small bowl and cover.
Full power (100%)
For a whole fruit, 150 g/5 oz, allow 15 seconds. Stand for 5 minutes, prick with fork and allow a further 15 seconds. *Do not over-heat in the initial frozen state as it may explode. Watch very carefully.*
For 175 g/6 oz slices, allow 1 minute. Separate with knife. Stand, covered, for 5 minutes.
For grated rind, allow 5 to 10 seconds or until thawed.

Juice   *To thaw*
Use a small jug or basin, uncovered
Full power (100%)
For 2 cubes (from ice tray), allow 1 minute; 4 cubes, allow 2 minutes. Stir.

LETTUCE
Although soups and dishes containing cooked lettuce can be frozen, lettuce itself is unsuitable for freezer storage as it goes limp and slimy, due to its high water content.

LIVER
See **Beef, Chicken, Lamb, Pork, and Turkey**

LOBSTER
See **Crab**

LOGANBERRIES
See **Blackberries**

M

MACARONI
See **Pasta**

MANGE TOUT (SNOW PEAS or SUGAR PEAS)
Select fresh mange tout and discard any which are damaged. Top and tail. Blanch for 2 minutes. Cool, drain and pack.

Freezer storage   12 months

To thaw and cook
Use a large bowl; cover
Full power (100%)
For 225 g/8 oz, allow 5 minutes, stirring halfway through.

MANGOES
Label with weight of fruit before preparation if using dry sugar method – thawing time is calculated on this. Remove skin. Slice or cut into pieces and discard stone. Use either the **dry sugar** or **sugar syrup** method.

Freezer storage   12 months

Dry sugar   *To thaw*
Use a medium bowl; cover
Full power (100%)
Two, unskinned weight, 450 g/1 lb each: Allow 4 minutes. After 3 minutes, remove thawed pieces. Gently separate with a knife and continue thawing. Stand, covered, for 5 to 10 minutes or until thawed.

Sugar syrup   *To thaw*
Use a medium bowl; cover
Full power (100%)
For 450 g/1 lb prepared mango, allow 2 minutes. Gently separate with a fork and continue for a further 1 minute. Stand, covered, for 10 to 15 minutes or until thawed.

MARGARINE
Treat as for **Butter**.

Freezer storage   3 to 6 months, depending on type (e.g. salted or unsalted).

MARROW
(and the rest of the Squashes)
Because of the quantity of water in these vegetables they are best frozen after cooking. Cook, drain and mash, then cool and pack.

Baby marrows: treat these as for **Courgettes**

Freezer storage 12 months

To thaw and heat
Use a medium bowl; cover
Full power (100%)
For 450 g/1 lb, allow 5 minutes or until heated through, breaking up with a fork after 3 minutes.

MELONS
Due to the high water content, frozen melon tends to soften. Use in fruit salads or compotes. Weigh melon, note unprepared weight on freezer label. Halve, remove seeds. Cut into wedges, pare flesh from peel; slice or dice. Use the **dry sugar** method.

Freezer storage 12 months

Dry sugar *To thaw*
Use a medium bowl; cover
Full power (100%)
Weight before preparation, 1.5 kg/3¾ lb; allow 4 minutes. Gently break up with a fork, halfway through. Stand, covered, for 10 to 15 minutes or until thawed.

MILK
Homogenised cows' milk or goats' milk is suitable for freezing, but never in glass bottles as these are likely to shatter with the expansion of the contents. Leave headspace to allow for expansion. The milk may separate on thawing but whisking if heating can help to improve it. Semi-skimmed and skimmed milk both freeze well in their cartons.

Freezer storage 1 month

To thaw
Use a jug, uncovered
Full power (100%)
For 300 ml/½ pint, allow 1½ minutes. Break up with a fork and allow a further 30 seconds. Whisk if necessary and stand for 10 minutes, or until any ice has thawed. To heat this quantity, continue on Full power, after breaking up with a fork, for 4½ minutes, or until as hot as desired, whisking halfway.

MUFFINS
Freeze cooked. Interleave with grease-proof paper, or clear film before packing to stop them sticking together.

Freezer storage 1 month

To thaw and heat
Stand on a piece of kitchen paper towel, uncovered
Full power (100%)
For 1 muffin allow 10 to 15 seconds, then slice and toast in the usual way.

MUSHROOMS
Mushrooms tend to soften when frozen, so are only suitable for cooking. Do not blanch as this may toughen them. Wipe, leave whole or slice. **Open-freeze** then pack.

Sautéed mushrooms Allow 65 g/2½ oz butter or margarine to 450 g/1 lb mushrooms. Slice, season with salt, pepper and lemon juice and fry briskly on a conventional hob until any liquid has evaporated and the mushrooms are lightly browned. Cool and pack.

Freezer storage 3 months

Whole raw *To thaw and cook*
Use a small bowl; cover
Full power (100%)
For 125 g/4 oz, allow 3 minutes. Drain off juice halfway through and stir.

Sliced raw *To thaw and cook*
Use a small bowl; cover
Full power (100%)
For 125 g/4 oz, allow 2½ minutes. Drain off juice halfway through.

Sautéed mushrooms
To thaw and heat
Use a small bowl; cover
Full power (100%)
For 125 g/4 oz, allow 2 minutes, or until heated through.

MUTTON
Treat as for **Lamb**

N

NECTARINES
Treat as for **Apricots**

O

OFFAL
See **Beef, Lamb, Pork** and **Veal**

ONIONS
Onions are readily available and store well; it seems a waste of space to freeze them. If frozen, they must be very well wrapped to prevent their odour permeating other foods. Small onions and pickling onions can be frozen whole after removing the skins. For large onions, remove skins; chop or slice. **Blanch** for 3 minutes. Cool, drain and pack.

Freezer storage   6 months

Sliced   *To thaw*
Use a medium bowl; cover
Full power (100%)
For 450 g/1 lb, allow 5 to 6 minutes or until thawed, stirring halfway through.

Whole small onions   *To thaw*
Use a medium bowl; cover
Full power (100%)
For 450 g/1 lb, allow 3½ minutes. Re-arrange after 2 minutes. Stand, cover-ed, for 15 minutes or until thawed.

ORANGES
Treat as for **Lemons**
For segments, treat as for **Grapefruit**

Seville oranges   Buy during their short season and make marmalade when convenient, allowing extra fruit to counteract loss of pectin, as is neces-sary when making jam with frozen fruit. Remove any stalk ends, scrub skins thoroughly, then slice, remove pips and use the **dry sugar** or **sugar syrup** method for freezing. Reduce the quantity of sugar required in the mar-malade recipe according to the amount used in the freezing method.
For thawing, see **Grapefruit**.

OXTAIL
See **Beef**

P

PANCAKES
See **Batters**

PARSNIPS
Use young fresh parsnips. Peel or scrub, slice or dice. Blanch for 5 minutes. Cool, drain and pack. Older parsnips are best cooked and mashed before freezing.

Freezer storage   12 months

Sliced or diced   *To thaw and cook*
Use a medium bowl; cover
Full power (100%)
For 450 g/1 lb, allow 11 minutes or until tender, breaking up and stirring halfway through.
Mashed   *To thaw and heat*
Use a medium bowl; cover
Full power (100%)
For 450 g/1 lb, allow 5 minutes or until heated throughout, breaking up with a fork after 3 minutes.

PARTRIDGE
Ready-frozen birds should be taken home to the freezer as quickly as pos-sible to avoid thawing; *no thawed bird should be re-frozen without cooking it first*. Over-wrap before placing in the freezer.

Fresh birds   Do not remove feathers before hanging; hang birds by the neck. Allow about one week. The ideal temperature for hanging is between 4° to 7°C/39° to 45°F. Usually the bird is ready if the feathers can be easily plucked from the tail. Pluck, draw, wash and dry. Wrap well. Freeze giblets separately (see below).

Freezer storage   6 months

To thaw
Place on a plate; cover
Power setting (50%)
Allow 6 to 7 minutes per 450 g/1 lb, turning over halfway through. Stand, covered, for 20 to 25 minutes or until thawed.

Giblets Wash the heart, livers, gizzard and neck in salt water. Rinse in fresh water. Dry and pack.

Freezer storage 3 months

To thaw
Place in a small bowl; cover.
Power setting (50%)
For 325 g/12 oz, allow 2 minutes. Stand, covered, for 10 minutes or until thawed.

PASTA
Cook pasta, cool and pack. Make flat packs of cooked pasta (any type) or rice in heatproof bags. It is very easy to thaw and reheat in the same bag in the microwave cooker.

Freezer storage 6 months

Tagliatelle, macaroni, spaghetti, noodles etc. *To thaw and heat*
Full power (100%)
For 225 g/8 oz, allow 3 minutes, then transfer to a large bowl. Pour over 600 ml/1 pint boiling water, cover and allow 5 minutes or until hot. After 3 minutes, check and gently separate.

Flat packs *To thaw and heat*
Prick the bag to prevent it bursting on heating. Place on a shallow plate.
Full power (100%)
For 225 g/8 oz, allow 3 to 4 minutes. Shake bag halfway through cooking.

PASTRY
Choux pastry Freeze unfilled. Cook, cool and pack in boxes. Thaw and fill when required.

Freezer storage 3 months

Thaw at room temperature, although fully thawed pastry is not as crisp as freshly baked choux pastry. (Crisp in a hot oven; leave to cool before filling.)

Flaky pastry Freeze this uncooked. Shape before freezing, or leave in a block pack and thaw and use as required.

Freezer storage 3 months

To thaw
Stand on a plate, uncovered

Full power (100%)
For 225 g/8 oz, allow 30 seconds. Check frequently to ensure that it does not over-soften. Stand, covered, for 5 minutes or until thawed. Small shapes can be baked in a conventional oven straight from frozen.

Hot water crust pastry Not suitable for freezing. Cooked pies *can* be frozen but the pastry loses crispness. Very short storage times are recommended as so many types of fillings are used and their freezer life affects the quality of the thawed product.

Freezer storage 1 week

Thaw at room temperature

Puff and Rough Puff pastry Store uncooked. Shape before freezing, or leave in a block and use as required.

Freezer storage 3 months

To thaw
Treat as for **Flaky pastry**

Shortcrust pastry Freeze uncooked. Shape, leave in a block or make up small pastries like patties, sausage rolls and mince pies. If a filling is to be used, brush the inside surface of the pastry with a little oil, melted butter or egg white. Thicken fruit juice fillings with cornflour.

Freezer storage 3 months

To thaw
Treat as for **Flaky pastry**. Small filled patties, pies and sausage rolls: Bake from frozen in a conventional oven.

Suet pastry Uncooked suet pastry can be frozen but is so quick to make that it is not worth freezing.

Suet puddings Conventionally cooked meat and fruit suet puddings should be cooled and tightly wrapped before freezing. Microwave-cooked puddings are not suitable for freezing as the pastry hardens on reheating.

Freezer storage 1 month

To thaw and heat
Place in a container which fits the pudding shape and cover. Stand a cup of cold water in the cooking cavity next to the pudding as this helps slow down the process.
Full power (100%)
For a 450 g/1 lb steak pudding, allow $7\frac{1}{2}$ minutes. Remove cover and check that the meat is piping hot by inserting a knife to the base of the pudding. Serve at once, before the crust hardens.

PAW PAW
Treat as for **Mango**

PEACHES
Treat as for **Apricots**

PEARS
Choose ripe, but not over-ripe pears. Peel, slice or quarter and remove cores. Use the **dry sugar** or **sugar syrup** method.

Freezer storage   12 months

Quartered in dry sugar   *To thaw*
Use a medium bowl; cover
Full power (100%)
For 450 g/1 lb, allow 2 minutes. Stand for 10 minutes.

To thaw and cook, allow 7 minutes. Rearrange halfway through. Stand, covered, for 3 minutes or until thawed.
Sugar syrup   *To thaw*
Use a medium bowl; cover
Full power (100%)
For 450 g/1 lb, allow 2 minutes. Gently break up with a fork and continue for 1 minute more. Stand, covered, for 10 to 15 minutes or until thawed. Cooking is not recommended as there is far more syrup than would normally be used and the fruit disintegrates into the liquid. For cooking, drain the pears after thawing, replace in the medium bowl and cook, covered, for $4\frac{1}{2}$ minutes or until tender, rearranging halfway.

PEAS (Fresh)
Discard any pods that are no longer tender. Pod, discarding blemished peas. **Blanch** for 1 minute, shaking the wire basket during blanching to allow the peas to heat evenly. Cool, drain and pack.

Freezer storage   12 months

To thaw and cook
Use a medium bowl; cover
Full power (100%)
For 225 g/8 oz, allow 8 minutes or until tender, stirring halfway through.

PEPPERS (Capsicums)
Halve, remove core and seeds. Slice, chop, dice or leave in halves. **Blanch** for 3 minutes, cool, drain and pack. (Peppers can be frozen unblanched but will have a shorter storage life.)

Freezer storage
Blanched: 12 months
Unblanched: 6 months

To thaw
Sliced, chopped and diced
Use a medium bowl; cover
Full power (100%)
For 225 g/8 oz, allow $3\frac{1}{2}$ minutes. Break up and stir halfway through. Stand, covered, for 5 minutes.

Halves   Place on a plate; cover
Full power (100%)
For 2 halves, allow 3 minutes, rearranging halfway through. Stand, covered, for 5 minutes or until thawed.

PHEASANT
Treat as for **Partridge**

PINEAPPLE
Weigh fruit and note down the unprepared weight on the freezer label. The thawing times are based on this weight. Peel and core; cut into slices or chunks. Cover with fresh or bought orange juice with 1 tablespoon lemon juice added. Stir in sugar to taste, if liked. Stand overnight in a refrigerator before freezing.

Freezer storage   12 months

To thaw
Use a large bowl; cover
Full power (100%)
For 900 g/2 lb weight before prepara-

tion, allow 7 minutes. Gently separate with a knife halfway through. Stand, covered, for 10 minutes or until thawed.

PLUMS
Treat as for **Damsons**

PORK
Almost all pork products are suitable for freezing but they do not generally keep as long as other meat. Salted or pickled pork does not freeze well.

Chops Prepare as for joints. Interleave meat with greaseproof paper to allow for easier separation when frozen. or **open-freeze**, then pack in large strong bags for easy access to one or two at a time.

Freezer storage 6 months

To thaw
Place on a plate or shallow dish with the thin ends towards the centre. Cover with kitchen paper towel.
Power settings (50%) and Defrost (30%)
Allow 4 minutes on 50%. Reduce power to Defrost (30%) and allow 10 minutes per 450 g/1 lb. Separate, if necessary, halfway through (sooner if only thawing one or two chops). Chops vary in thickness, so check frequently and remove thawed ones as soon as possible.

Joints Wipe meat with a clean cloth. Remove any extra fat. Pad any bones with extra wrapping and wrap well. Never stuff boneless joints before freezing; stuffing ingredients cut down storage life of the meat – and can lead to problems if insufficiently thawed before cooking. Over-wrap.

Freezer storage
Fresh pork: 6 months
Salted or pickled pork: 1 month

To thaw
Stand meat on trivet or upturned plate in a shallow dish. Cover. Shield thin ends with small pieces of foil.

Power settings 50% and Defrost (30%)
Leg, fillet end, knuckle, rolled loin, rolled belly and rolled leg etc. Allow 10 minutes on 50%. Reduce power to Defrost (30%) and allow 12 minutes per 450 g/1 lb. Turn over once during thawing. Wrap in foil and stand for 1 hour or until thawed. For pork fillet, allow 30 minutes standing time. Meat should be completely thawed before cooking.

Hearts Must be absolutely fresh. Wash well and remove tubes; trim off fat. Pack and freeze as soon as possible.

Freezer storage 3 months

To thaw
Use a shallow dish; cover
Full power (100%)
For 275 g/10 oz prepared weight, allow 2 minutes. Stand, covered, for 10 minutes or until thawed.

Kidneys Must be absolutely fresh. Wash and remove cores, trim off fat. Large kidneys should be sliced or diced. Pack and freeze as soon as possible.

Freezer storage 3 months

To thaw
Use a small bowl; cover
Full power (100%)
For 325 g/12 oz, allow 2 minutes. Gently separate with a fork. Allow a further 30 seconds. Stand, covered, for 10 minutes or until thawed.

Liver Must be absolutely fresh. Wash and trim; slice and interleave. Pack in containers and freeze as soon as possible.

Freezer storage 3 months

To thaw
Use a shallow dish or small bowl; cover
Full power (100%)
For 225 g/8 oz, allow 2 to 2½ minutes, separating after 1 to 2 minutes. Stand, covered, for 8 minutes or until thawed.

Mince Use freshly minced pork and pack and freeze as soon as possible. Make flat packages to save time at the thawing stage.

Freezer storage 3 months

To thaw
Use a large bowl; cover
Power settings 50% and Defrost (30%)
Give 5 minutes on 50%. Reduce power to Defrost (30%) and allow 12 minutes per 450 g/1 lb, breaking up frequently with a fork to speed up the thawing.

Pigs trotters Clean well. Wrap separately. Pack.

Freezer storage 3 months

To thaw
Place on a plate, uncovered
Full power (100%)
For 4 trotters, allow 3 minutes. Rearrange and allow a further 30 seconds. Stand for 10 to 15 minutes or until thawed.

Pig's head Does not freeze well due to its high water content.

Sausages Avoid freezing in a block as they are difficult to separate. Interleave with greaseproof paper before packing, or **open-freeze**.

Freezer storage 3 months

To thaw
Arrange sausages on a plate. Cover with a kitchen paper towel.
Full power (100%)
For 225 g/8 oz give 2½ minutes. Remove any sausages which are almost thawed. Stand 3 to 4 minutes before cooking. Cook conventionally. *Never fry in the microwave.*

Stewing pork Trim off fat and gristle, cut into cubes or neat pieces. Pack.

Freezer storage 6 months

To thaw
Use a medium bowl; cover
Full power (100%)
For 450 g/1 lb, allow 4 minutes, breaking up and stirring halfway through

thawing. Stand, covered, for 5 to 10 minutes or until thawed.

Tongue Must be absolutely fresh; keeps longer if unsalted. Wipe the tongue with a clean cloth. Trim and wrap well.

Freezer storage
Unsalted: 3 months
Salted: 1 month

To thaw
Use a medium bowl; cover
Full power (100%)
For 400 g/14 oz, allow 2 minutes. Separate, then stand, covered, for 15 minutes or until thawed.

POTATOES
Potatoes require cooking before freezing, otherwise they turn black.

New potatoes Scrape, or scrub skins and leave on. Boil until tender in the usual way, toss in butter, cool, pack.

Freezer storage 3 months

To thaw and heat
Use a medium bowl; cover
Full power (100%)
For 450 g/1 lb, allow 7 minutes or until thoroughly heated through, rearranging halfway.

Maincrop potatoes Peel or scrub and cook as required; they are best frozen cooked and mashed as Duchesse or croquette potatoes, as baked jacket potatoes, roast potatoes, or blanched chips.

Freezer storage 6 months

Mashed *To thaw and heat*
Use a medium bowl; cover
Full power (100%)
For 450 g/1 lb, allow 5 minutes. Break up with a fork after 3 minutes.

Duchesse potatoes Peel, cook and mash with butter and milk. Pipe on to a piece of greaseproof paper on a tray. **Open-freeze** then pack, or cook in a conventional oven. Cool. **Open-freeze** then pack.

Freezer storage 6 months

Duchesse (not browned)
To thaw
Place in a circle on a plate, uncovered
Full power (100%)
For 8 Duchesse potatoes (weighing about 450 g/1 lb in total), allow 2½ minutes. Brown in a preheated conventional oven.

Duchesse (oven-browned)
To thaw and heat
Place in a circle on a plate, uncovered
Full power (100%)
For 8 Duchesse potatoes (about 450 g/1 lb total weight), allow 4½ minutes or until heated through. The potatoes are not as crisp after heating. If preferred, they can be crisped in a preheated conventional oven.

Croquettes Peel, cook, make into croquettes, then egg-and-crumb. **Open-freeze,** then pack.

Freezer storage 6 months

To thaw
Place in a circle on a plate, uncovered
Full power (100%)
For 8 croquettes (about 325 g/12 oz total weight), allow 2½ minutes. Turn over halfway through. Fry conventionally to achieve a crisp finish. *Never fry in a microwave cooker.*

Jacket potatoes Scrub, prick and cook. Cut in half, scoop out and mash. Refill potatoes. (Include a filling, provided it is suitable for freezing. Check the main ingredients in this A–Z.) **Open-freeze,** then pack.

Freezer storage
Mashed – without an extra filling: 6 months
Mashed – with a filling: check filling with this A–Z section
(E.g. unsmoked bacon has a storage life of 2 to 3 weeks. This would then be the storage time for jacket potatoes with chopped unsmoked bacon.)
To thaw and heat
Place on a plate, uncovered
Full power (100%)
For two halves, filling uppermost

(400 g/14 oz total weight), allow 6 minutes, rearranging halfway through.

Chips **Blanch** uncooked chips in hot fat for 3 minutes on a conventional hob. Drain, cool and pack. (Cooked chips do not give such good results when frozen as they lose crispness). *Never fry in a microwave cooker.*

Freezer storage 6 months

To thaw
Arrange on a flat plate, uncovered
Full power (100%)
For 450 g/1 lb, allow 3 minutes. Spread the chips evenly over the plate, leaving a space in the centre. Rearrange halfway through. Cook conventionally.

Roast potatoes Cool. **Open-freeze,** then pack.

Freezer storage 6 months

To thaw and heat
Arrange in a circle on a plate, uncovered
Full power (100%)
For 8 potatoes (225 g/8 oz total weight) allow 3½ minutes or until heated through, rearranging halfway through heating. The potatoes are not crisp like freshly roasted ones but if they were lightly roasted before freezing they can be plunged into deep hot fat on the conventional hob to crispen.

PRAWNS
Select only firm prawns. If uncooked, boil in salted water for 5 minutes. Cool and pack with or without shells. If freezing bought prawns, ensure that they are absolutely fresh and have not been previously frozen. Freeze with or without shells.

Freezer storage 1 month

To thaw
Place in a shallow dish, uncovered
Full power (100%)
For 450 g/1 lb in a block, allow 11 to 12 minutes. For loose prawns, allow 7 to 8 minutes. Break up the block or stir halfway. Stand, uncovered, for 10 to 15 minutes or until thawed.

54

PUMPKINS

Choose a top-quality pumpkin and only freeze when cooked. After cooking, drain and mash; cool and pack.

Freezer storage   12 months

To thaw and heat
Use a medium bowl; cover
Full power (100%)
For 450 g/1 lb, allow 5 minutes or until heated through, breaking up with a fork after 3 minutes.

Q

QUINCE

With only small quantities available commercially, quince is generally cooked, then added to dishes which include other cooked fruit. But if you have a supply of fresh fruit, cook in the usual way, cool, pack.

Freezer storage   12 months

To thaw and heat
Follow the instructions for the type of recipe in which quince has been included. Or use to make jam.

R

RABBIT
Joints See **Chicken**

Domestic rabbits should be hung according to taste before skinning. Wild rabbits have to be gutted and skinned the moment they are shot or the flesh develops a rank flavour. Joint, soak in cold salted water for at least 2 hours. Rinse, pat dry and pack with extra protection for the sharp ends of the legs.

Freezer storage   6 months

To thaw
Use a large bowl; cover
Full power (100%)
For 900 g/2 lb in portions, allow 9 minutes, rearranging the pieces halfway through. Stand, covered, for 15 minutes or until thawed.

RADISHES

Not suitable for freezing as they lose their crispness.

RASPBERRIES
See **Blackberries**

REDCURRANTS
See **Blackcurrants**

RHUBARB

Select young, thin pink sticks. Wipe with a clean cloth. Remove tops and tails; cut sticks into 2.5-cm/1-inch pieces. Pack straight into strong bags for free flow access. OR **blanch** for 1 minute, cool, drain and pack into strong bags. OR use the **dry sugar** method. Cooked poached or stewed rhubarb is suitable for freezing.

Freezer storage   12 months

Dry sugar   *To thaw and cook*
Use a large bowl; cover
Full power (100%)
For 450 g/1 lb, allow 12 minutes or until tender, stirring once or twice.
Stewed   *To thaw and heat*
Use a large bowl; cover
Full power (100%)
For 450 g/1 lb, allow 10 minutes or until heated through, stirring once or twice.

RICE

Cook rice, cool and pack. Make flat packs of cooked rice in heatproof bags. It is very easy to thaw and reheat in the same bag in the microwave cooker.

Freezer storage   3 months

To thaw and heat
Use a large bowl; cover
Full power (100%)
For 225 g/8 oz, allow 9 minutes or until heated through, break up and stir after 3 and 6 minutes. For flat packs, puncture bag, place on a shallow dish or plate and allow 3 to 4 minutes for the same quantity to thaw and reheat.

RUM and BRANDY BUTTER
See **Brandy or Rum Butter**

S

SALMON
See **Fish**

SALSIFY
Choose young, tender, unblemished roots. Scrub – do not peel. **Blanch** whole for 2˙minutes. Peel if desired, while still warm. Cut into 5 to 7.5-cm/2 to 3-inch strips. Cool, drain and pack.

Freezer storage   12 months

To thaw and cook
Use a medium bowl; cover
Full power (100%)
For 450 g/1 lb, allow 13 minutes or until tender, gently separating halfway through.

SAUSAGES
See **Beef, Pork** and **Veal**

SCALLOPS
Buy absolutely fresh, remove from shells and discard the black beards. Wash in salt water, dry and pack.

Freezer storage   1 month

To thaw
Use a small bowl; cover
Full power (100%)
For 225 g/8 oz, allow 1½ minutes. Gently separate and allow a further 30 seconds. Stand, covered, for 10 minutes or until thawed.

SEAKALE
Treat as for **Celery**

Freezer storage   12 months

SEVILLE ORANGES
See **Oranges**

SHRIMPS
Treat as for **Prawns**

Freezer storage   1 month

SMOKED SALMON
See **Fish**

56

SORBETS
See **Ice Cream**

Freezer storage   3 months

SPAGHETTI
See **Pasta**

SPINACH
Choose good-quality leaves. Remove stalks. Wash and shake dry. **Blanch** for 2 minutes. To avoid the leaves sticking together, blanch a few at a time. Cool and pack. Or cook the spinach as usual. Cool, drain, squeeze out excess moisture. Pack.

Freezer storage   12 months

Blanched   *To thaw and cook*
Use a medium bowl; cover
Full power (100%)
For 225 g/8 oz, allow 8 minutes, breaking up and stirring several times.

Cooked   *To thaw and heat*
Use a medium bowl; cover
Full power (100%)
For 225 g/8 oz, allow 5 minutes or until heated through, breaking up halfway through.

STEAK AND KIDNEY
See **BEEF**
Treat as for **Stewing Beef**

STRAWBERRIES
Strawberries lose their firmness when frozen and are only suitable for use in desserts and fruit salads. Select only perfect ones. Hull and **open-freeze**, or slice and use the **dry sugar** or purée methods, or open-freeze slices.

Freezer storage   12 months

Dry sugar   *To thaw*
Use a medium bowl; cover
Full power (100%)
For 450 g/1 lb, allow 2½ minutes. Gently rearrange after 1 and 2 minutes. Leave to stand, covered, for 5 to 10 minutes or until thawed.
Purée   *To thaw*
Use a small bowl; cover

Full power (100%)
For 225 g/8 oz, allow 2 minutes, breaking up with a fork after 1 and 2 minutes, or until thawed.
Open-frozen   *To thaw*
Strawberries hold their shape better if thawed at room temperature. Stand them on kitchen paper towel. If liked, served partially thawed.

SWEDES
Choose young, small swedes. Label bags with unprepared (i.e. bought) weight if freezing raw. See thawing instructions. Peel, thickly slice or dice. **Blanch** for 5 minutes. Drain, cool and pack. Older swedes are best cooked, mashed and cooled quickly before freezing.

Freezer storage   12 months

Sliced or diced   *To thaw and cook*
Use a medium bowl; cover
Full power (100%)
For 900 g/2 lb weight before preparation, allow 12 minutes or until tender, stirring halfway through.

Mashed   *To thaw and heat*
Use a medium bowl; cover
Full power (100%)
For 450 g/1 lb, allow 5 minutes or until heated through, breaking up with a fork after 3 minutes.

SWEETBREADS
See **Lamb** or **Veal**

SWEETCORN
Freeze just-ripe, plump-looking corn cobs. Remove husk, silk and stalk. **Blanch** small cobs for 4 minutes, medium for 5 minutes, large for 6 minutes. Cool, drain and pack. Wrap each corn cob separately. Corn kernels should be blanched for 2 minutes, cooled, drained and packed. Leave headspace when packaging to allow for expansion.

Freezer storage   12 months

Corn kernels   *To thaw and cook*
Place in a shallow dish; cover
Full power (100%)
For 175 g/6 oz, allow 3 to 4 minutes.

Break up and stir with a fork halfway through.

Corn on the cob   *To thaw and cook*
Wrap individually in greaseproof paper or parchment and stand on a plate.
Full power (100%)
For 2, allow 6 to 8 minutes. Rearrange halfway through.

T

TAGLIATELLE
See **Pasta**

TOMATOES
Tomatoes should be fresh, just ripe and in peak condition. When thawed, they can only be used for cooking as they are soft, but the flavour is still that of fresh tomatoes. Wash, remove stalk, leave whole, slice or cut into quarters. Pack.

Juice   Wash tomatoes, liquidise and sieve. Pack, leaving half an inch of headspace for expansion.
For longer storage, choose ripe tomatoes, cut into pieces, simmer for 6 to 10 minutes until soft, then sieve, cool and pack, leaving headspace for expansion.

Pulp   Skin and halve tomatoes, removing hard cores. Cook gently until they soften and turn into juice. Sieve or liquidise, cool, pack, leaving headspace for expansion.
Salt or sugar can be added to juice and pulp. When sieving, use a nylon or hair sieve as a metal one can taint the tomatoes.

Freezer storage
Whole fresh tomatoes: 12 months
Juice (cooked): 12 months
Juice (uncooked): 1 month
Pulp: 12 months
The skin on whole frozen tomatoes will split and can be removed easily by holding the tomato under the cold water tap for a few seconds.

Whole tomatoes *To thaw and cook*
Place in a shallow dish; cover
Full power (100%)
For 4 whole tomatoes, allow 4 to 5
minutes. After 15 to 30 seconds, gently
separate them and arrange in a circle.
Prick skins, if necessary, to avoid burst-
ing. Continue cooking until tender, re-
moving them as they cook.
For 8 halves, allow 3 to 4 minutes.
Check and remove any cooked ones.

Frozen juice and pulp *To thaw*
Use a jug, uncovered
Full power (100%)
For 300 ml/$\frac{1}{2}$ pint, allow 2 minutes,
breaking up with a fork halfway
through. Stir before standing for 10 to
15 minutes or until thawed.

TONGUE
See **Beef** and **Lamb**

TRIPE
See **Beef**

TROUT
See **Fish**

TURKEY
Treat as for **Chicken**

Freezer storage   12 months

Whole bird *To thaw*
Stand on a trivet or upturned plate
standing in a shallow dish. Shield thin
parts with foil.
Full power (100%)
Allow 7 to 8 minutes per 450 g/1 lb.
Cover with kitchen paper towel.
Remove the giblets as soon as possible.
Turn over three times during thawing.
Immerse in cold water for 30 minutes
after thawing to ensure the bird is
completely thawed. Remove, drain and
dry. Cook only when it has completely
thawed and no ice is present.

Giblets Wash in salt water, rinse in
fresh water, pat dry and pack.

Freezer storage   3 months

To thaw
Use a medium bowl; cover

Full power (100%)
Allow 2 minutes. Separate and stand
for 10 to 15 minutes or until thawed.

Livers Must be absolutely fresh.
Can be separated from giblets before
freezing a whole turkey. Wrapped
separately they can be stored until
enough are saved for a pâté.

Freezer storage   3 months

To thaw
Use a small bowl; cover
Full power (100%)
For 325 g/12 oz, allow 1 minute.
Gently separate with a fork. Allow a
further 30 seconds. Stand, covered, for
10 to 15 minutes or until thawed.

TURNIPS
Choose young turnips. Peel, slice or
dice, then **blanch** for 5 minutes. Cool,
drain and pack.

Freezer storage   12 months

To thaw and cook
Use a medium bowl; cover
Full power (100%)
For 450 g/1 lb, allow 11 minutes or
until tender, stirring halfway through.

V

VEAL
All veal products are suitable (though
salted meat does not freeze well).

Brains Must be absolutely fresh.
Wash in salt water, snip off any pieces
of bone and all the fibres and any
membrane. Dry and pack.

Freezer storage   3 months

To thaw
Use a medium bowl; cover
Defrost (30%)
For 175 g/6 oz, allow 4 minutes, turning over after 2 and 3 minutes. Stand,
covered, for 5 to 10 minutes or until
thawed. Use at once.

Chops and escalopes Treat as for
joints (below). Interleave meat with

greaseproof paper to allow for easier separation when frozen. Or **open-freeze** and then pack.

Freezer storage 9 months

To thaw
Place separated pieces on a plate with thin parts to the centre, uncovered.
Power settings 50% and Defrost (30%)
Allow 5 minutes on 50%. Reduce power to Defrost (30%), then allow 10 minutes per 450 g/1 lb.

Hearts Must be absolutely fresh. Wash and remove tubes, trim off fat. Pack and freeze as soon as possible.

Freezer storage 3 months

To thaw
Place in a shallow dish; cover
Full power (100%)
For 325 g/12 oz, allow 2 minutes. Stand, covered, for 10 minutes or until thawed.

Joints Wipe the meat with a clean cloth. Remove any extra fat. Pad bones with extra wrapping, wrap well. Never stuff boneless joints before freezing; health hazards could occur if stuffing is not thawed out before cooking or not cooked through before serving.

Freezer storage 9 months

To thaw
Stand meat on a trivet or upturned plate in a shallow dish; cover. Protect thin ends with foil.
Power settings 50% and Defrost (30%)
Allow 10 minutes on 50%. Reduce power to Defrost (30%) and allow 12 minutes per 450 g/1 lb. Turn over once during thawing. Wrap in foil and stand for 1 hour. *The meat must be completely thawed before cooking.*

Kidney Must be absolutely fresh. Wash and remove cores, trim off fat. Pack and freeze as soon as possible.
Freezer storage 3 months

To thaw
Use a small bowl; cover

Full power (100%)
For 325 g/12 oz, allow 1 minute. Gently separate with a fork. Allow a further 30 seconds. Stand, covered, for 10 to 15 minutes or until thawed.

Liver Must be absolutely fresh. Wash and trim or wash, trim, slice and interleave. Pack in containers and freeze as soon as possible.

Freezer storage 3 months

To thaw
Use a shallow dish or bowl; cover
Full power (100%)
For 225 g/8 oz, allow 2 to $2\frac{1}{2}$ minutes, separating after 1 or 2 minutes. Stand, covered, for 8 minutes or until thawed.

Sausages See **Pork**

Freezer storage 3 months

To thaw
Arrange the sausages on a plate. Cover with a kitchen paper towel.
Full power (100%)
For 225 g/8 oz, allow $2\frac{1}{2}$ minutes. Remove any sausages once almost thawed. Stand for 3 to 4 minutes before cooking. Cook conventionally. *Never fry in the microwave.*

Stewing veal Trim off any fat and gristle; cut into cubes. Pack.

Freezer storage 3 months

To thaw
Place in a medium bowl; cover
Full power (100%)
For 450 g/1 lb, give 4 minutes, stirring halfway through. Stand, covered, for 5 to 10 minutes or until thawed.

Sweetbreads Must be absolutely fresh. Wash in salt water; dry; pack.

Freezer storage 3 months

To thaw
Place in a medium bowl, cover
Full power (100%)
For 225 g/8 oz, allow 1 minute. Separate and stand, covered, for 15 minutes or until thawed.

VENISON

Ready-frozen venison should be transported to the freezer as quickly as possible; *thawed meat should not be refrozen unless cooked.* Over-wrap. For fresh meat: wipe with a clean cloth, pad bones with extra wrapping; wrap well. Never stuff boneless joints before freezing; health hazards occur if stuffings thaw insufficiently before cooking.

Freezer storage   6 months

Joint   *To thaw*
Place on a plate, cover
Power setting 50%
For 1½ to 2½ kg/3 to 5 lb, allow 7 to 9 minutes per 450 g/1 lb. Stand, covered, for 1 hour or until thawed.

Pieces   *To thaw*
Use a large bowl; cover
Power setting 50%
For 900 g/2 lb pieces, allow 7 to 8 minutes per 450 g/1 lb. Stand, covered, for 15 to 20 minutes or until thawed.

W

WATERCRESS

Not recommended for freezing except in soups and other recipes.

WOOD PIGEON
See **Partridge**

Y

YEAST and YEAST PRODUCTS
Also see **Bread**
Cut fresh yeast into 25 g/1 oz pieces. Wrap in foil.

Freezer storage   1 month

To thaw
Yeast should be thawed at room temperature, as microwaving can kill it and the dough will fail to rise.

Yeast-based cakes, buns and pastries   (Brioche, Danish pastries)

Leave in their original wrappings and over-wrap, or wrap individually in foil for extra protection.

Freezer storage   4 to 6 weeks

To thaw
Place on paper towel, uncovered.
Full power (100%)
The timing depends on the size and density of the product. For one cake or bun, allow 10 to 15 seconds, then check to see if it is thawed. It should be warm to the touch if serving warm. If serving cold, remove after 10 seconds and leave to stand at room temperature. Should the food be over-heated, it will harden on cooling as too much moisture has been lost. Beware if heating products with jam fillings as the *jam heats more quickly than the pastry.*

YOGURT

Homemade yogurt is not suitable for freezing as the texture changes. Commercially frozen yogurt can be stored in the freezer in its carton or package. Whole-fruit, fruit-flavoured and stirred-type yogurt can be frozen in rigid containers, but leave headspace.

Freezer storage
Fruit yogurt: 3 months
Natural yogurt: 2 months

To thaw
Leave in the carton or place in a small bowl, uncovered
Full power (100%)
For 175 g/6 oz carton, allow 30 seconds. Beat well with a fork. Stand, uncovered, for 25 to 30 minutes.

YORKSHIRE PUDDINGS
See **Batters**

Z

ZUCCHINI
See **Courgettes**

Chapter 4

Soups and Starters

These recipes have been developed and tested on a microwave cooker with a 700-watt output. See page 20 if you have a cooker with a lower output (i.e. wattage). When reheating fish, meat and poultry dishes, always make quite sure they are piping hot throughout before serving.

CONSOMME

(Clear Beef Soup)

For 4 to 6

This clear soup is full of the goodness extracted from the meat, so the meat is not really suitable for re-use in another dish. This soup can be frozen.

PREPARATION: About 15 minutes, excluding straining
COOKING: About 59 minutes
SETTING: Full power (100%) and Defrost (30%)

325 g/¾ lb beef, free from fat, skin and sinews removed, minced
2 egg whites, lightly whisked
¼ level teaspoon salt
½ level teaspoon beef extract (e.g. Bovril)
1.2 litres/2 pints hot beef stock
75 ml/2½ fl oz dry sherry
2 hard-boiled egg whites cut into tiny fancy shapes, to garnish

1 Place the meat, raw egg whites, salt and beef extract in a large bowl. Whisking all the time, pour on the hot stock. Cook, covered, on Full power for 5 minutes or until boiling.
2 Reduce to Defrost (30%). Cook, uncovered, for 45 minutes to extract as much goodness from the meat as possible.
3 Strain carefully through a scalded jelly cloth. Stir in the sherry. Reheat on Full power (100%) for 9 minutes or until boiling, stirring halfway through heating.
4 Place the egg-white shapes in the bottom of a warmed tureen. Pour the consommé over the garnish.
Freezing: Freeze before garnishing. Use within 6 months.
Thawing: Full power (100%). Use a large bowl and cook, covered, for 25 minutes or until boiling, breaking up and stirring after 15 and 20 minutes.

TURKEY NOODLE SOUP

For 4 to 6

Any cooked game or poultry can be used instead of turkey. It is suitable for freezing.

PREPARATION: About 10 minutes
COOKING: About 14 minutes
SETTING: Full power (100%)

1 garlic clove, crushed
1 medium onion, peeled and finely chopped
1.2 litres/2 pints hot chicken stock
50 g/2 oz noodles
¼ teaspoon vegetable oil
225 g/8 oz cooked turkey, finely chopped
Salt and pepper to taste

1 Place the garlic and onion in a large bowl. Cover and cook for 3 minutes or until the onion is tender.
2 Stir in the hot chicken stock, noodles and oil. Cover and cook for 7 minutes to soften the noodles, stirring halfway through cooking.
3 Stir in the turkey and season with salt and pepper to taste. Cover and cook for 4 minutes, or until the turkey is hot and the noodles are quite soft, stirring halfway through cooking.
Freezing: Use within 6 months.
Thawing: Full power (100%). Use a large bowl. Cook, covered, for 25 minutes or until boiling, breaking up and stirring after 15 and 20 minutes.

ITALIAN SOUP

For 4 to 6

This is similar to minestrone and makes a substantial starter; it can also be served as a dish on its own, sprinkled with grated cheese, and a hunk of wholemeal bread. It is suitable for freezing.

PREPARATION: About 15 minutes
COOKING: About 21 minutes
SETTING: Full power (100%)

25 g/1 oz butter or margarine
1 small onion, peeled and coarsely chopped
125 g/4 oz finely shredded cabbage
1 celery stick, finely chopped
½ yellow pepper, seeds removed and finely diced
2 tablespoons frozen peas
1 carrot, peeled and thinly sliced
125 g/4 oz potato, peeled and diced
2 garlic cloves, crushed
25 g/1 oz macaroni
397 g/14 oz can of tomatoes, with juice
600 ml/1 pint hot beef stock
1 rounded tablespoon tomato purée
1 level tablespoon mixed dried herbs, or 2 tablespoons chopped fresh herbs
Salt and pepper to taste

1 Place the butter or margarine, onion, cabbage, celery, pepper, peas, carrot, potato and garlic in a large bowl. Cook, covered, for 11 minutes or until the vegetables are tender, stirring halfway through cooking.
2 Stir in the macaroni, tomatoes with their juice, the hot stock, purée, herbs and salt and pepper to taste. Cook, covered, for 10 minutes or until the macaroni is cooked through.
3 Pour into four warm serving bowls.

Freezing: Use within 6 months.
Thawing: Full power (100%). Use a large bowl. Cook, covered, for 25 minutes or until boiling, gently breaking up after 15 minutes and stirring well after 20 minutes.

CARROT AND ORANGE SOUP

For 4

A delightful soup which can be served either hot or cold. Chill after cooking, but before adding the garnish. It is suitable for freezing – or it can be stored, uncovered, in the refrigerator.

PREPARATION: About 10 minutes
COOKING: About 20 minutes
SETTING: Full power (100%)

575 g/1¼ lb carrots, peeled and thinly sliced
1 medium onion, peeled and chopped
1 level teaspoon mixed dried herbs, or 2 teaspoons chopped fresh herbs
1 level teaspoon caster sugar
25 g/1 oz butter or margarine
Finely grated rind of 1 orange
150 ml/¼ pint unsweetened orange juice (see method)
600 ml/1 pint hot chicken stock
Salt and pepper to taste
Finely grated carrot, to garnish

1 Place the carrot, onion, herbs, sugar, butter or margarine and orange rind into a large bowl. Cook, covered, for 15 minutes or until the vegetables are tender, stirring halfway through cooking.
2 Stir in the orange juice, stock, and salt and pepper to taste. (If using the juice from the orange, squeeze it into a measuring jug and add only enough unsweetened orange juice to make it up to 150 ml/¼ pint.) Cook, covered, for 5 minutes or until boiling.

3 Put through a liquidiser or food processor. Pour into four warm soup bowls and garnish each with a little finely grated carrot.
Freezing: Freeze before garnishing. Use within 6 months.
Thawing: Full power (100%). Use a large bowl. Cook, covered, for 25 minutes or until boiling, breaking up and stirring after 15 and 20 minutes.

CELERY AND CARAWAY SOUP
For 6

The caraway seeds can be omitted if you don't happen to like them. The soup is suitable for freezing.

PREPARATION: About 10 minutes
COOKING: About 21 minutes
SETTING: Full power (100%)

450 g/1 lb head of celery, washed and finely sliced
1 medium onion, peeled and finely chopped
25 g/1 oz butter or margarine
1 rounded tablespoon plain flour
600 ml/1 pint milk
600 ml/1 pint hot chicken stock
1 level teaspoon dried mixed herbs
Celery salt and pepper to taste
1 to 2 teaspoons caraway seeds (optional)
6 celery leaves, to garnish

1 Place the celery, onion and butter or margarine in a large bowl. Cover and cook for 10 minutes or until vegetables are tender, stirring halfway through cooking.
2 Stir in the flour, blend in the milk, half the hot stock, herbs, celery salt and pepper to taste. Cover and cook for 7 minutes or until boiling, stirring halfway through cooking.
3 Add the remaining stock and put through a liquidiser or food processor.

Stir in the caraway seeds. Cook, uncovered, for 4 minutes or until boiling, stirring halfway through cooking.
4 Pour into six warm soup bowls and garnish each with a celery leaf.
Freezing: Freeze before garnishing. Use within 6 months.
Thawing: Full power (100%). Use a large bowl and cook, covered, for 25 minutes or until boiling, breaking up and stirring after 15 and 20 minutes.

CHILLED CUCUMBER SOUP
For 4

A delicious summer soup – and an easy starter for a dinner party. It is suitable for freezing or it can be stored overnight, uncovered, in the refrigerator.

PREPARATION: About 10 minutes, plus chilling
COOKING: About 15½ minutes
SETTING: Full power (100%)

2 cucumbers, weighing 1.25 kg/ 2¼ lb, peeled and roughly chopped
1 medium onion, peeled and roughly chopped
50 g/2 oz butter or margarine
50 g/2 oz cornflour
300 ml/½ pint cold milk
450 ml/¾ pint cold chicken stock
Salt and white pepper to taste
150 ml/¼ pint double cream
Thin slices of cucumber, to garnish

1 Put the cucumber and onion through a liquidiser or food processor. Transfer to a large bowl and add the butter or margarine. Cook, covered, for 11 minutes or until the vegetables are tender, stirring halfway through.
2 Mix the cornflour to a paste with a little of the cold milk and gradually

add the rest of the milk, half the stock, and salt and pepper to taste. Cook, uncovered, for 4½ minutes or until thickened and boiling, stirring every minute.
3 Add the remaining stock. Put through a liquidiser or food processor until smooth. Use a sieve if an even smoother soup is desired.
4 Stir in the cream, check and adjust the seasoning. Refrigerate until chilled, then garnish with slices of cucumber before serving.
Freezing: Freeze after step 3. Use within 6 months.
Thawing: Full power (100%). Use a large bowl. Cook, covered, for 25 minutes or until boiling, breaking it up and stirring halfway through thawing. Continue as above, from step 4.

WATERCRESS SOUP
For 4

A delicately flavoured soup which can be served hot or cold. Chill after cooking and stir in 4 tablespoons of cream to add richness. The soup is suitable for freezing, or it may be stored, overnight, uncovered, in the refrigerator.

PREPARATION: About 10 minutes
COOKING: About 16 minutes
SETTING: Full power (100%)

450 g/1 lb potatoes, peeled and thinly sliced

3 tablespoons water
25 g/1 oz butter or margarine
2 bunches of watercress, washed and trimmed, if necessary
450 ml/¾ pint water
1 egg yolk, lightly beaten
300 ml/½ pint milk
Salt and ground white pepper to taste
4 sprigs of watercress, to garnish

1 Place the potatoes and 3 tablespoons of water in a large bowl. Cook, covered, for 6 minutes or until the potatoes are partially cooked.
2 Stir the potatoes, add the butter or margarine and watercress. Cook, covered, for 6 minutes or until the potatoes are tender, stirring halfway through cooking. Add the 450 ml/½ pint water.
3 Put the soup through a liquidiser or food processor with the egg yolk and work until smooth. Stir in the milk, and salt and pepper to taste.
4 Return to the bowl. Cook, covered, for 4 minutes or until boiling, stirring halfway through cooking.
5 Pour into four warm soup bowls. Garnish with sprigs of watercress.
Freezing: Freeze before garnishing. Use within 6 months.
Thawing: Full power (100%). Use a large bowl and cook, covered, for 25 minutes or until boiling, breaking up and stirring after 15 and 20 minutes.

HOT SPICY DIP WITH CRISP RAW VEGETABLES
For 6 or more

A simple recipe to serve with drinks before dinner, as a starter, or as part of a buffet. The dip is suitable for freezing.

PREPARATION: About 15 minutes
COOKING: About 9 minutes

SETTING: Full power (100%)

DIP

1 medium onion, peeled and
finely chopped
1 garlic clove, crushed
25 g/1 oz butter or margarine
25 g/1 oz plain flour
240 ml/8 fl oz tomato juice
1 tablespoon white wine vinegar
2 tablespoons Worcestershire
sauce
1 tablespoon soy sauce
Salt and pepper to taste
1 level teaspoon prepared
wholegrain English mustard

VEGETABLES

3 large carrots, peeled and
sliced into neat sticks
1 large green pepper, seeds
removed, cut into strips
3 sticks celery, cut in half
lengthways and cut into
strips

1 Put the onion with the garlic and
butter or margarine into a medium
bowl. Cook, covered, for 5 minutes
or until the vegetables are tender,
stirring halfway through cooking.
2 Stir in the flour. Gradually blend
in the tomato juice, vinegar,
Worcestershire sauce, soy sauce and
salt and pepper to taste. Cook,
uncovered, for 4 minutes until
thickened and hot, stirring after
every minute.
3 Put the mixture through a
liquidiser or food processor until
smooth, then stir in the mustard.
4 Serve in a warm bowl, with the
raw vegetables arranged separately
to be eaten with the dip.
Freezing: Freeze the dip only and
use within 6 months. Prepare the
vegetables when required.
Thawing: Full power (100%). You
need a small bowl. Cook, covered, for
5 minutes or until completely heated
throughout, breaking up and stirring
after 2 and 4 minutes.

66

MUSHROOM PATE
Makes 4 generous helpings

*This pâté makes an interesting starter
and can also be used as a sandwich
spread. It is suitable for freezing. Use
well-flavoured dark mushrooms.*

PREPARATION: About 10 minutes,
plus chilling
COOKING: About 5 minutes
SETTING: Full power (100%)

$\frac{1}{2}$ level teaspoon dried rosemary,
well pounded, or $\frac{1}{4}$ teaspoon
powdered rosemary
1 garlic clove, crushed
50 g/2 oz butter or margarine
225 g/8 oz mushrooms, finely
sliced
Salt and pepper to taste
75 g/3 oz full fat cream cheese
50 g/2 oz fresh white
breadcrumbs
Small triangles of toast or fried
bread and sprigs of parsley,
to garnish

1 Put the rosemary into a medium
bowl with the garlic, butter or
margarine and mushrooms. Cook,
covered, for 5 minutes or until the
mushrooms are tender, stirring
halfway through cooking. Put the
mixture through a liquidiser or food
processor until smooth.
2 Stir in the salt and pepper to taste,
the cheese and the breadcrumbs.
Spoon into four small ramekin dishes
and smooth over the tops. Refrigerate
for 2 to 3 hours or until chilled.
3 Garnish around the edges with tiny
toast or fried bread triangles. Place a
sprig of parsley in the centre of each
ramekin.
Freezing: Freeze before garnishing.
Use within 3 months.
Thawing: Full power (100%).
Arrange the dishes in a circle. Cook,
uncovered, for 2 minutes to soften,
then stand for 20 minutes or until
completely thawed.

Chapter 5
Fish and Shellfish

COD WITH TWO-CHEESE SAUCE
For 4

For a change, instead of Cheese sauce use a Herb sauce (page 118) or a Barbecue sauce (page 118). This is not suitable for freezing as the sauce turns thin and watery during thawing.

PREPARATION: About 10 minutes
COOKING: About 9½ minutes, plus grilling time
SETTING: Full power (100%) and conventional grill

4 fresh or frozen cod steaks, 675 g/1½ lb total weight

SAUCE
25 g/1 oz butter or margarine
25 g/1 oz plain flour
300 ml/½ pint milk
1 level teaspoon prepared French mustard
Salt and pepper to taste
40 g/1½ oz finely grated Parmesan cheese mixed with:
40 g/1½ oz Gruyère cheese, coarsely grated
Sprigs of parsley, to garnish

1 Place the cod steaks in a shallow dish with the narrow ends towards the centre. Cover and cook for 4 minutes, or until the flesh flakes easily and looks opaque. If frozen fish is used, cook for a further 3 minutes (or until the flesh flakes easily and is opaque). Set aside, covered.
2 Put the butter or margarine in a large jug. Cook, uncovered, for 1 minute or until melted. Blend in the flour. Stir in the milk, mustard, salt and pepper to taste. Cook, uncovered, for 3 minutes or until thickened, stirring every minute. Beat in half the cheese.
3 Place the fish steaks in a shallow fireproof dish. Cook, covered, for 1½

minutes or until the fish is hot. Pour over the sauce.
4 Sprinkle over the remaining cheese and brown under a conventional preheated grill. Garnish with sprigs of parsley.
Freezing: Not suitable.

SPICY FISH
For 4

If the spicy taste is not what you like, omit the Worcestershire sauce. This recipe is not suitable for freezing as the fish breaks up and the sauce is difficult to stir during thawing.

PREPARATION: About 15 minutes
COOKING: About 20 minutes
SETTING: Full power (100%)

1 tablespoon olive oil or vegetable oil
1 large onion, peeled and finely chopped
1 green pepper, seeds removed, finely diced
1 carrot, peeled and finely sliced
400 g/14 oz can of tomatoes with juice, chopped
1 level teaspoon mixed dried herbs, or 2 teaspoons chopped fresh herbs
Salt and pepper to taste
¼ teaspoon anchovy essence
2 teaspoons Worcestershire sauce
4 fresh or frozen haddock or cod fillets, 225 g/8 oz each

1 Put the oil, onion, pepper and carrot into a medium bowl. Cook, covered, for 8 minutes or until the vegetables are tender.
2 Stir in the tomatoes and juice, the herbs, and salt and pepper to taste. Add the anchovy essence and Worcestershire sauce, if using. Set aside, covered.
3 Arrange the haddock or cod fillets in a shallow dish. Fold the thinnest

68

part of the fillet under each piece of fish. Cover and cook for 7 minutes, rearranging halfway through cooking, until the flesh flakes easily and looks opaque. If frozen fish is used, cook for a further $3\frac{1}{2}$ minutes (or until the flesh flakes easily and looks opaque).
4 Pour off the fish juices. (If fresh fish was used, freeze these cooking juices to use as stock for another dish.) Spoon the vegetable sauce over the fish and cook, uncovered, for $5\frac{1}{2}$ minutes or until the fish is heated throughout.
Freezing: Not suitable.

FRESH MACKEREL IN WINE SAUCE
Serves 2 to 4

Makes an excellent starter for 4 or a main course for 2. You can use 150 ml/$\frac{1}{4}$ pint unsweetened orange juice instead of the wine. This dish is suitable for freezing.

PREPARATION: About 10 minutes, plus 2 to 3 hours marinating time
COOKING: About 10 minutes
SETTING: Full power (100%)

4 mackerel fillets, 575 g/1$\frac{1}{2}$ lb total weight
150 ml/$\frac{1}{4}$ pint dry white wine
Juice of 1 orange
Rind of 1 orange, removed with a zester
150 ml/$\frac{1}{4}$ pint water
25 g/1 oz butter
25 g/1 oz plain flour
Salt and pepper to taste
Twists of sliced orange, to garnish

1 Lay the fillets out flat in a large shallow casserole dish, 23 by 23 by 6 cm/9 by 9 by 2$\frac{1}{2}$ inches. Mix together the wine, orange juice, orange rind and water. Pour over the fish and leave to marinate for 2 to 3 hours.

2 Drain the marinade into a measuring jug, then make up the quantity to 300 ml/$\frac{1}{2}$ pint with more water. Set aside, covered, while making the sauce.
3 Cover and cook the fish for 5$\frac{1}{2}$ minutes or until the flesh flakes easily and looks opaque. Rearrange the fillets halfway through cooking, then set aside, still covered, while making the sauce.
4 Place the butter in a large jug. Cook for 1 minute or until melted, then stir in the flour. Gradually blend in the wine liquor. Cook, uncovered, for 4 minutes or until thickened, stirring every minute. Season with salt and pepper.
5 Gently lift the fish on to a warm serving plate. Pour the sauce over and garnish with twists of orange.
Freezing: Freeze after step 4, leaving them in the shallow dish. Use within 1 month.
Thawing: Full power (100%). Cook, covered, for 25 minutes or until the sauce and fish are both completely heated throughout. Turn the dish around halfway through cooking.

SMOKED MACKEREL KEDGEREE
For 4

A substantial main course: Cooked, flaked, smoked haddock can be used instead of mackerel. It can be frozen, but without the hard-boiled eggs, as cooked eggs tend to take on a rubbery texture when frozen.

PREPARATION: About 10 minutes
COOKING: About 16 minutes, plus 7 minutes standing time
SETTING: Full power (100%)

325 g/12 oz long-grain rice
750 ml/1$\frac{1}{4}$ pints cold fish or chicken stock
$\frac{1}{4}$ teaspoon oil

$\frac{1}{4}$ level teaspoon salt
1 level tablespoon mixed dried
  herbs, or 2 tablespoons finely
  chopped fresh herbs
2 hard-boiled eggs, roughly
  chopped
50 g/2 oz butter or margarine,
  cut into knobs
Freshly ground pepper to taste
450 g/1 lb cooked smoked
  mackerel, flaked

1 Put the rice, stock, oil, salt and
herbs into a large bowl. Cook, covered,
until the stock comes to the boil, then
cook for 12 minutes; do not stir.
Leave to stand, covered, for 7 minutes
to finish cooking.
2 Stir the hard-boiled eggs, butter or
margarine and pepper to taste into
the rice. Stir in the flaked mackerel.
Cook, covered, for 4 minutes or until
the mackerel is hot, stirring halfway
through cooking.
Freezing: Freeze after step 1. Use
within 1 month.
Thawing: Full power (100%). Use a
large bowl. Cook, covered, for 12
minutes or until completely heated
throughout. Break up with a fork and
stir after 6 minutes. Then continue at
step 2 above.

SALMON STEAKS WITH LIME MAYONNAISE
For 4

*A delightful summer main course and
one that's easy to prepare. The
mayonnaise can be made in advance and
stored in the refrigerator for 1 week.
For a change, serve the salmon with
Hollandaise sauce (page 118). The dish
is not suitable for freezing as the
mayonnaise separates and the salmon
tends to toughen during thawing.*

PREPARATION: About 15 to 20
  minutes

70

COOKING: About 5 minutes, plus 5
  minutes standing time
SETTING: Full power (100%)

4 fresh or frozen salmon steaks,
  800 g/1$\frac{3}{4}$ lb total weight

MAYONNAISE
2 egg yolks
$\frac{1}{4}$ level teaspoon salt
$\frac{1}{4}$ level teaspoon caster sugar
$\frac{1}{2}$ level teaspoon prepared
  French mustard
150 ml/$\frac{1}{4}$ pint olive oil
1 tablespoon lime juice
White pepper to taste
Twists of sliced lime and sprigs
  of fresh dill, to garnish

1 Arrange the salmon steaks on a
large plate with the narrow ends
towards the centre. Cover and cook
for 5 minutes; if frozen fish is used,
cook for a further 3 minutes.
Rearrange them halfway through
cooking, then stand, covered, for 5
minutes or until the flesh flakes easily
and looks opaque. Remove the cover
and leave the fish to cool.
2 To make the mayonnaise: Put the
egg yolks, salt, caster sugar and
mustard in a bowl and beat them
together.
3 Add the oil, drop by drop, to the
mixture, beating well all the time.
Continue in this way until the sauce
thickens: At this stage, the oil can be
added more quickly.
4 Once half the oil has been added,
beat in a little lime juice. Beat in the
remaining oil, then add the rest of
the juice. Season with pepper.

5 Spoon the mayonnaise over the salmon and garnish with twists of sliced lime and sprigs of fresh dill.
Freezing: Not suitable.

SOLE WITH BROWN BUTTER
For 4

This dish could be served as a starter for 6. Instead of brown butter, serve with Hollandaise sauce (page 118) or Barbecue sauce (page 118). It is not suitable for freezing as the fish tends to toughen during thawing.

PREPARATION: About 10 minutes
COOKING: About 6 minutes, plus frying time
SETTING: Full power (100%) and conventional hob

12 fresh, frozen or thawed sole fillets, 675 g/1½ lb total weight, skinned
Salt and pepper to taste
Finely grated rind of 2 lemons
175 g/6 oz unsalted butter
2 tablespoons white wine vinegar
Twists of lemon, to garnish

1 Sprinkle the fish fillets with salt and pepper to taste and lemon rind. Roll up and secure with wooden cocktail sticks. Place the fish in a shallow casserole dish. Cook, covered, for 6 minutes or until the flesh flakes easily and looks opaque. Rearrange halfway through cooking.
2 Meanwhile, melt the butter in a frying pan on the conventional hob until the butter is light brown but not scorched. Stir in the vinegar.
3 Drain the sole, remove the wooden cocktail sticks and arrange the fish on a warm serving dish. Pour over the butter and serve at once. Garnish with twists of lemon.
Freezing: Not suitable.

PRAWN CURRY
For 4

This is a mild curry to serve with plain boiled rice and traditional side dishes of sliced tomatoes, desiccated coconut, sliced bananas and mango chutney. It is suitable for freezing, but only if the prawns have not been frozen before use; they should not be re-frozen.

PREPARATION: About 10 minutes
COOKING: About 18 minutes
SETTING: Full power (100%)

50 g/2 oz butter or margarine
1 large onion, peeled and finely chopped
2 garlic cloves, crushed
1 rounded tablespoon plain flour
1 tablespoon tomato purée
$\frac{1}{4}$ level teaspoon salt
1 teaspoon Worcestershire sauce
1 level tablespoon curry powder
$\frac{1}{4}$ level teaspoon ground cumin
$\frac{1}{4}$ level teaspoon mild or hot chilli powder, or to taste
25 g/1 oz creamed coconut
450 ml/$\frac{3}{4}$ pint hot fish or vegetable stock
450 g/1 lb peeled fresh prawns or thawed frozen prawns
Chopped fresh parsley, to garnish

1 Put the butter or margarine, onion and garlic in a medium bowl and cook, covered, for 7 minutes or until the onion is tender, stirring halfway through cooking.
2 Stir in the flour, tomato purée, salt, Worcestershire sauce, curry powder, cumin, chilli powder, creamed coconut and hot stock. Cook, uncovered, for 8 minutes to allow the flavours to develop, stirring halfway through cooking.
3 Stir in the prawns and cook, uncovered, for 3 minutes or until the prawns are hot, stirring halfway

through cooking. Garnish with chopped parsley.
Freezing: Freeze before garnishing. Use within 1 month.
Thawing: Full power (100%). Use a medium bowl. Cook, covered, for 12 minutes or until the prawns are completely heated through. Gently break up after 7 minutes and stir.

POTTED GARLIC SHRIMPS
For 4

This is an easy recipe to prepare and makes a good starter. It is suitable for freezing, but only if the shrimps have not been frozen before use as they should not be refrozen. The dish may be stored overnight in the refrigerator.

PREPARATION: About 5 minutes
COOKING: About 2½ minutes, plus refrigeration time
SETTING: Full power (100%)

2 garlic cloves, crushed
175 g/6 oz butter, cut into pieces
325 g/12 oz fresh or thawed shrimps, peeled
A pinch of cayenne pepper
Pepper to taste
Sprigs of parsley, to garnish

1 Put the garlic and butter into a small bowl. Cook, uncovered, for 2½ minutes or until butter has melted.
2 Stir in the shrimps, cayenne pepper and pepper to taste. Spoon into four small ramekin dishes. Refrigerate until set, then garnish with sprigs of parsley.
Freezing: Freeze in the ramekin dishes. Use within 1 month.
Thawing: Full power (100%). Place the ramekin dishes on a plate. Cook for 30 seconds then leave to stand for 30 minutes to 1 hour, or until thawed. The exact thawing time will depend upon the room temperature.

MUSSELS COOKED IN WHITE WINE
For 2

If you need more than 2 servings, use a conventional cooking method as a larger container is difficult to accommodate in the microwave cooker. This recipe is not suitable for freezing as the mussels lose their texture and toughen during thawing.

PREPARATION: About 20 minutes
COOKING: About 10 minutes
SETTING: Full power (100%)

1.2 litres/2 pints fresh mussels
25 g/1 oz butter or margarine
2 shallots, peeled and finely chopped
1 small onion, peeled and finely chopped
1 level tablespoon chopped fresh parsley
1 teaspoon lemon juice
180 ml/6 fl oz dry white wine
Black pepper to taste

1 Discard any mussels which are not tightly closed. Scrub well and remove any weeds or barnacles. Carefully remove any tufts, hair or beard with a sharp knife. Wash well in cold water. Set aside.
2 Put the butter or margarine, shallots, onion and parsley into a large bowl. Cook, covered, for 3 minutes or until the onion is tender, then stir in the lemon juice, wine and pepper to taste. Cook, covered, for a further 2 minutes or until the liquid is boiling.
3 Toss in the mussels. Cook, covered, for 5 minutes or until the shells open; toss the mussels halfway through cooking.
4 Pile into a warm serving dish and pour over the liquor. Serve with crisp rolls.
Freezing: Not suitable.

Chapter 6
Poultry
and Game

CHICKEN BREASTS WITH LEMON SAUCE
For 4

Ring the changes with a Herb sauce (page 118) or a Barbecue sauce (page 118). Frozen chicken breasts can be used but they must be thawed out first to ensure the meat is thoroughly cooked. This dish is suitable for freezing.

PREPARATION: About 10 minutes
COOKING: About 10 minutes
SETTING: Full power (100%)

4 chicken breasts, 575 g/1¼ lb
   total weight

SAUCE
25 g/1 oz butter or margarine
25 g/1 oz plain flour
150 ml/¼ pint dry white wine
150 ml/¼ pint hot chicken stock,
   less 2 tablespoons
Finely grated rind of 1 lemon
2 tablespoons lemon juice
Salt and pepper to taste
Lemon slices and sprigs of fresh
   parsley, to garnish

1 Arrange the chicken breasts around a medium bowl. Cook, covered, for 6 minutes or until tender, rearranging the pieces halfway through cooking. Set aside, covered.

2 For the sauce, place the butter or margarine in a large jug. Cook, uncovered, for 1 minute or until melted. Stir in the flour. Gradually blend in the wine, stock, lemon rind, lemon juice, and salt and pepper to taste. Cook, uncovered, for 3 minutes or until thickened, stirring after every minute.

3 Arrange the chicken on a warm serving dish. Spoon the sauce over and garnish with slices of lemon and sprigs of parsley.

Freezing: Freeze before garnishing. Use within 6 months.

Thawing: Full power (100%). Use a large bowl. Cook, covered, for 15 minutes or until the liquid is boiling and the chicken is completely heated throughout. Separate the chicken pieces halfway through heating and gently stir the sauce.

CHICKEN PAPRIKA
For 4

Frozen chicken breasts can be used, but they must be thawed before use to ensure the meat is thoroughly cooked. This is suitable for freezing.

PREPARATION: About 15 minutes
COOKING: About 25 minutes
SETTING: Full power (100%)

4 chicken breasts, 675 g/1½ lb
   total weight
75 g/3 oz bacon, without rind
   and coarsely chopped
1 large onion, peeled and finely
   sliced
125 g/4 oz button mushrooms
25 g/1 oz butter or margarine
225 g/8 oz tomatoes, skinned
   and roughly chopped
25 g/1 oz plain flour
300 ml/½ pint hot chicken stock
2 level tablespoons mild
   paprika powder
Salt and pepper to taste
4 tablespoons soured cream
3 kiwi fruit, peeled and sliced
   and chopped fresh parsley,
   to garnish

1 Place the chicken in a large shallow dish. Cover and cook for 8 minutes or until tender, rearranging the pieces halfway through cooking. Set aside, covered.

2 Put the bacon in a large bowl; add the onion, mushrooms, butter or margarine and tomatoes. Cover and cook for 10 minutes or until tender, stirring halfway through cooking.

3 Stir in the flour, blend in the hot stock, the paprika powder and salt

and pepper to taste. Add the chicken.
Cook for 5 minutes or until the sauce
has thickened, stirring halfway
through cooking.
4 Stir in the cream and cook,
uncovered, for about 1 minute.
Arrange the kiwi fruit around the dish
and serve, sprinkled with parsley.
Freezing: Freeze before garnishing.
Use within 6 months.
Thawing: Full power (100%). Use a
large bowl. Cook, covered, for 20
minutes or until the liquid is boiling
and the chicken is thoroughly heated
through. Break up after 6 minutes,
rearrange the chicken and stir after a
further 8 minutes.

CHICKEN TANDOORI-STYLE
For 4

*The 'tandoor' is the traditional oven
used to cook this aromatic spiced
chicken. However, we are using a
microwave – the secret is in the
marination of the chicken. Frozen
chicken breasts can be used for this but
they must be thawed before use to ensure
the meat is thoroughly cooked. Don't
freeze it as the chicken toughens during
thawing and its appearance is not
improved. Serve with plain boiled rice.*

PREPARATION: About 10 minutes,
  plus 24 hours marinating in
  refrigerator
COOKING: About 12 minutes, plus
  grilling time
SETTING: Full power (100%) and
  conventional grill

1 garlic clove, peeled and finely
  chopped
A 5 cm/2 inch piece of fresh
  ginger, peeled and finely
  chopped
Ground black pepper to taste
¼ level teaspoon salt
1 level teaspoon chilli powder
½ level teaspoon ground cumin

1 level teaspoon ground
  coriander
Finely grated rind and juice of
  1 lemon
4 chicken breasts, 800 g/1¾ lb total
  weight, skinned
4 tablespoons natural yogurt
Fresh coriander leaves, or
  cucumber slices, lemon
  wedges and spring onion
  curls, to garnish

1 Pound together the garlic, ginger,
pepper to taste, salt, chilli powder,
cumin, coriander, lemon rind and
juice in a pestle and mortar, or place
the ingredients in a bowl and crush
with the end of a wooden rolling pin.
2 Make 3 or 4 diagonal slashes across
each chicken breast. Rub each breast
with the spice mixture and arrange in
a shallow fireproof dish. Spoon a
tablespoon of yogurt over each breast.
3 Refrigerate for 24 hours, covering
the dish so the aroma does not penetrate
any other food. Turn the chicken over
several times during marination.
4 Place the dish in the microwave
and cook, covered, for 12 minutes or
until tender, turning the chicken
pieces over halfway through cooking.
5 Place the drained chicken under a
preheated grill to brown.
6 Garnish with fresh coriander, or
cucumber, lemon and spring onion,
and serve with rice or salad.

Freezing: Not suitable.

CHICKEN WITH MUSHROOMS AND GREEN PEPPER
For 4

*Frozen chicken legs can be used, but
they must be thawed first to ensure the
meat is thoroughly cooked. The dish is
suitable for freezing.*

PREPARATION: About 15 minutes

COOKING: About 20 minutes, plus
grilling time
SETTING: Full power (100%) and
conventional grill

4 chicken legs, 900 g/2 lb total
weight
2 medium onions, peeled and
finely sliced
125 g/4 oz button mushrooms,
thinly sliced
1 large green pepper, seeds
removed, thinly sliced
1 garlic clove, crushed
25 g/1 oz plain flour
150 ml/¼ pint tomato juice
300 ml/½ pint hot chicken stock
2 tablespoons lemon juice
1 tablespoon Worcestershire
sauce
½ level teaspoon dried chopped
thyme, or 1 teaspoon chopped
fresh thyme
Salt and pepper to taste

1 Put the chicken under a preheated
conventional grill until nicely brown
all over.
2 Meanwhile, put the onions,
mushrooms, green pepper and garlic
in a large bowl. Cook, covered, for 8
minutes or until the vegetables are
tender, stirring halfway through
cooking.
3 Stir in the flour. Gradually blend
in the tomato juice, stock, lemon
juice, Worcestershire sauce, thyme
and salt and pepper to taste.
4 Place the chicken in the bowl and
spoon over the sauce. Cook, covered,
for 12 minutes or until the chicken is
tender and the sauce is hot,
rearranging the chicken halfway
through cooking.

Freezing: Use within 6 months.

Thawing: Full power (100%). Put in
a large bowl. Cook, covered, for 25
minutes or until the liquid is boiling
and the chicken is completely heated
through. Break up and rearrange after
15 and 20 minutes.

76

CHICKEN DRUMSTICKS WITH TARRAGON
For 4

*For a different flavour, use parsley or
rosemary instead of tarragon. Try using
fresh herbs, in which case double the
quantity given for dried. Frozen chicken
thighs can be used, but they must be
thawed first to ensure the meat is
thoroughly cooked in the given time.
This dish is suitable for freezing.*

PREPARATION: About 10 minutes
COOKING: About 24 minutes
SETTING: Full power (100%)

1 medium onion, peeled and
chopped
1 garlic clove, crushed
2 level teaspoons dried tarragon
25 g/1 oz butter or margarine
25 g/1 oz plain flour
150 ml/¼ pint dry white wine
150 ml/¼ pint hot chicken stock
Salt and pepper to taste
8 chicken thighs, 900 g/2 lb total
weight
Sprigs of fresh tarragon, to
garnish

1 Put the onion, garlic, tarragon and
butter or margarine in a large bowl.
Cook, covered, for 4 minutes or until
the onion is tender.
2 Stir in the flour, then gradually stir
in the wine, stock, and salt and
pepper to taste. Add the chicken
thighs. Cook, covered, for 20 minutes
or until tender, taking care to stir and
rearrange the chicken pieces after 5
and 10 minutes.
3 Remove the chicken, place on a
warm serving dish and keep warm.
Put the sauce through a liquidiser or
blender.
4 Spoon a little sauce over the
chicken and serve the remaining sauce
separately. Garnish the dish with
sprigs of fresh tarragon. If freezing,

pour over all of the sauce, and do not garnish.
Freezing: Use within 6 months.
Thawing: Full power (100%). Use a large bowl. Cook, covered, for 20 minutes or until the liquid is boiling and the chicken is completely heated through. Gently break up after 5 minutes; rearrange after 10 minutes.

BRANDIED CHICKEN DRUMSTICKS
For 4

Dry red or white wine can be used instead of brandy. Frozen chicken drumsticks can be used but they must be thawed out first to ensure the meat is thoroughly cooked. The recipe can be frozen.

PREPARATION: About 10 minutes, plus 2 hours marinating time
COOKING: About $8\frac{1}{2}$ minutes, plus frying time
SETTING: Full power (100%) and conventional hob

8 drumsticks, 900 g/2 lb total weight, pricked with a fork
30 ml/1 fl oz brandy
50 g/2 oz butter or margarine
2 rounded tablespoons tomato purée
About 250 ml/8 fl oz hot chicken stock
25 g/1 oz plain flour
Salt and pepper to taste
Sprigs of fresh dill, parsley, or snipped chives, to garnish

1 Place the chicken in a large shallow dish. Sprinkle over the brandy and leave to stand for about 2 hours, turning the chicken over frequently during this time. Pour the brandy off into a measuring jug.
2 Melt 25 g/1 oz of the butter or margarine in a frying pan on the conventional hob. Fry the drumsticks until brown.

3 Arrange the drumsticks in the shallow dish and cook, covered, on Full power for 5 minutes or until tender. Set aside and keep warm.
4 Pour the chicken juices into the reserved brandy and stir in the tomato purée. Make up to 300 ml/$\frac{1}{2}$ pint with hot stock.
5 Place the remaining 25 g/1 oz butter or margarine in a large jug. Cook, uncovered, for 1 minute or until melted. Stir in the flour, then slowly blend in the stock. Cook, uncovered, for $2\frac{1}{2}$ minutes or until thickened, stirring every minute. Add salt and pepper to taste.
6 Place the drumsticks on a warm serving dish and spoon the sauce over. Garnish with sprigs of dill or parsley, or chives.
Freezing: Freeze before garnishing. Use within 6 months.
Thawing: Full power (100%). Use a large bowl. Cook, covered, for 15 minutes or until the liquid is boiling and the chicken is completely heated throughout. Rearrange the drumsticks after 10 minutes.

CHICKEN WITH FRESH PINEAPPLE
For 4

Use unsweetened canned pineapple if preferred, though it tends to soften and go stringy unless added later – see the method. This dish is suitable for freezing.

PREPARATION: About 15 minutes
COOKING: About 40 minutes
SETTING: Full power (100%) and Defrost (30%)

1 medium onion, peeled and finely chopped
2 medium carrots, peeled and thinly sliced into rings
$\frac{1}{2}$ large red pepper, seeds removed, finely diced

25 g/1 oz butter or margarine
675 g/1½ lb uncooked chicken
  flesh, coarsely diced
2 rings fresh pineapple, about
  5 mm/¼ inch thick, skin
  removed and each ring cut
  into 6 pieces
1 level teaspoon mixed dried
  herbs, or 2 teaspoons chopped
  fresh herbs
Salt and pepper to taste
25 g/1 oz cornflour
125 ml/¼ pint cold water
450 ml/¾ pint hot chicken stock
Fresh chopped parsley, to garnish

1 Put the onion, carrot, red pepper
and butter or margarine in a large
bowl. Cook, covered, on Full power
for 5 minutes, or until partially
cooked.
2 Stir in the chicken. Cook, covered,
on Full power for 10 minutes or until
heated through and starting to cook.
Stir halfway through cooking.
3 If using fresh pineapple, stir it in
now with the herbs, salt and pepper
to taste.
4 Blend the cornflour with the cold
water to make a smooth paste. Stir
into the chicken mixture with the hot
chicken stock.
5 Cook, covered, on Full power for 5
minutes or until boiling. Stir. (If
using canned pineapple, stir it in
now.) Reduce to Defrost (30%) and
cook, covered, for 20 minutes or until
the chicken is tender, stirring after 12
minutes and 15 minutes.
6 Spoon into a warm serving dish.
Garnish with chopped parsley.

Freezing: Freeze before garnishing; if
using canned pineapple, leave it out
until reheating the dish. Use within 6
months.

Thawing: Full power (100%). Place
in a large bowl. Cook, covered, for 20
minutes or until the liquid is boiling
and the chicken is heated throughout.
Break up and stir halfway through
cooking. Add canned pineapple at this
stage.

DUCK WITH FRUIT SAUCE

For 4

*A raspberry purée can be used instead of
the apple purée. Frozen duck joints can be
used, but they must be thawed before use
to ensure the meat is thoroughly cooked.
This recipe is suitable for freezing.*

PREPARATION: About 15 minutes
COOKING: About 19 minutes, plus
  grilling time
SETTING: Full power (100%) and
  the conventional grill

4 duck joints, 900 g/2 lb total
  weight
1 medium onion, peeled and
  finely chopped
50 g/2 oz butter or margarine
½ red pepper, seeds removed,
  finely diced
2 rounded tablespoons tomato
  purée
1 garlic clove, crushed
1 level teaspoon cornflour
150 ml/¼ pint dry red wine
300 ml/½ pint apple purée
Salt and pepper to taste
Sprigs of fresh rosemary or
  watercress, to garnish

1 Place the duck joints in a large
bowl. Cook, covered, for 9 minutes or
until tender, rearranging the joints
halfway through cooking.

2 Then brown the duck joints under
a pre-heated conventional grill.

3 Meanwhile, put the onion, butter
or margarine, pepper, tomato purée
and garlic into a medium bowl and
cook, covered, for 6 minutes or until
tender.

4 Blend the cornflour with the wine
and stir into the vegetables with the
apple purée, and salt and pepper to
taste. Cook, uncovered, for 4 minutes
or until thickened, stirring every
minute.

5 Put the cooked mixture through a liquidiser or food processor until smooth.

6 Arrange the duck on a warm serving dish. Pour the sauce over and garnish with sprigs of rosemary.

Freezing: Freeze before garnishing. Use within 3 months.

Thawing: Full power (100%). Place in a large bowl. Cook, covered, for 25 minutes or until the liquid is boiling and the duck is completely heated through. Gently separate and rearrange after 15 minutes.

TURKEY WITH MUSHROOM AND WINE SAUCE
For 4

Vermouth can be used instead of the wine, and frozen turkey breasts can be used — but they must be thawed before use to ensure that the meat is thoroughly cooked. The recipe is suitable for freezing.

PREPARATION: About 15 minutes
COOKING: About 38 minutes
SETTING: Full power (100%) and
   Defrost (30%)

1 medium onion, peeled and
   finely chopped
25 g/1 oz butter or margarine
1 garlic clove, crushed
300 ml/½ pint hot chicken stock
60 ml/2 fl oz dry white wine
Salt and pepper to taste
4 uncooked turkey breasts,
   675 g/1½ lb total weight
175 g/6 oz button mushrooms,
   finely sliced
25 g/1 oz cornflour
5 tablespoons single cream or
   milk

1 Place the onion, butter or margarine and garlic in a large bowl. Cook, covered, on Full power for 5 minutes or until tender. Stir in the stock, wine, and salt and pepper to taste. Put the mixture through a liquidiser or food processor until smooth. Set aside, covered.

2 Using the same large bowl, arrange the turkey breasts around the base and sides. Cook, covered, on Full power for 5 minutes or until the turkey breasts are heated through, rearranging them at the halfway stage.

3 Pour the vegetable sauce over the turkey. Cook, covered, on Full power for 10 minutes or until the sauce is boiling. Make sure that the turkey breasts are completely covered by the sauce during cooking.

4 Stir in the mushrooms. Reduce to Defrost (30%) and cook, covered, for 15 minutes or until the turkey breasts are tender.

5 Remove the turkey breasts and mushrooms with a slotted spoon and transfer to a warm serving dish; keep warm. Set aside a few mushrooms for garnish.

6 Place the cornflour in a large jug. Stir in the cream or milk to make a smooth paste, then gradually stir in the hot sauce. Increase to Full power (100%) and cook, uncovered, for 3 minutes or until the sauce is thickened, stirring after every minute.

7 Spoon some of the sauce over the turkey breasts and garnish with the reserved mushrooms. Serve the remaining sauce separately.

Freezing: If freezing, pour all the sauce over the turkey. Use within 6 months.

Thawing: Full power (100%). Use a large bowl. Cook, covered, for 15 minutes or until the liquid is boiling and the turkey is completely heated through. Separate the pieces halfway through heating.

TURKEY OLIVES
For 4

This is a very filling main course. Frozen turkey breasts can be used, but they must be thawed first to ensure the meat is thoroughly cooked. Chopped walnuts could be used instead of dates. This dish can be frozen.

PREPARATION: About 15 minutes
COOKING: About 10½ minutes
SETTING: Full power (100%)

4 uncooked turkey breasts, about 125 g/4 oz each, lightly beaten

STUFFING
1 small onion, peeled and quartered
2 rounded tablespoons tomato purée
5 tablespoons milk
1 level teaspoon chopped fresh herbs
Salt and pepper to taste
25 g/1 oz fresh white breadcrumbs

20 g/¾ oz stoned dates, finely chopped

SAUCE
25 g/1 oz butter or margarine
25 g/1 oz plain flour
A 225 g/8 oz can of tomatoes, with juice, sieved and made up to 300 ml/½ pint with chicken stock or water
Salt and pepper to taste
1 to 2 tablespoons double or whipping cream
Sprigs of fresh fennel or parsley, to garnish

1 For the stuffing, put the onion, tomato purée, milk, herbs and salt and pepper through a liquidiser or food processor until smooth. Stir in the breadcrumbs and dates.

2 Divide the mixture into four and spread over the centre of each turkey breast. Roll up and, if necessary, secure with wooden cocktail sticks.

3 Place the turkey olives around the edge of a shallow casserole, leaving a space between each. Cook, covered,

for 6 minutes or until tender, rearranging them halfway through cooking. Set aside, covered.

4 Now for the sauce: Place the butter or margarine in a large jug. Cook, uncovered, for 1 minute or until melted.

5 Stir in the flour. Gradually add the tomato liquid, salt and pepper. Cook, uncovered, for $3\frac{1}{2}$ minutes or until thickened, stirring every minute.

6 Stir in 1 to 2 tablespoons cream.

7 Arrange the 'olives' on a warm serving dish. Remove the cocktail sticks. Pour over the sauce and garnish the dish with sprigs of fresh fennel or parsley.

Freezing: Freeze before garnishing. Use within 6 months.

Thawing: Full power (100%). Use a medium bowl. Cook, covered, for 16 minutes or until the liquid is boiling and the turkey olives are completely heated through, separating and turning them over after 6 minutes.

BRAISED PIGEONS
For 4

Frozen pigeons can be used but they must be thawed first to ensure the meat is thoroughly cooked. The dish is not suitable for freezing as the texture of the flesh toughens during reheating.

PREPARATION: About 15 minutes
COOKING: About 1 hour 11 minutes
SETTING: Full power (100%) and Defrost (30%)

50 g/2 oz butter or margarine
1 level teaspoon chopped fresh tarragon
4 pigeons, cleaned and trussed, 2 kg/4 lb 6 oz total weight
1 medium onion, peeled and finely chopped
1 courgette, trimmed and thinly sliced
125 g/4 oz carrots, peeled and thinly sliced
2 tomatoes, skinned and roughly chopped
1 level teaspoon caster sugar
2 garlic cloves, crushed
4 cloves
1 rounded tablespoon tomato purée
Salt and pepper to taste
25 g/1 oz plain flour
150 ml/$\frac{1}{4}$ pint medium sherry
300 ml/$\frac{1}{2}$ pint hot chicken stock
4 small slices of bread, to fry
Sprigs of watercress, to garnish

1 Cream together the butter or margarine and tarragon. Divide into four and place a piece inside each bird. Arrange the birds in a shallow casserole dish, breast side down. Cook, covered, on full power for 7 minutes. Turn over and cook, uncovered, for 6 minutes or until tender. Set aside, covered.

2 In a large bowl, put the onion, courgette, carrots, tomatoes, sugar, garlic, cloves and tomato purée. Add salt and pepper to taste. Cook, covered, on full power for 8 minutes or until the vegetables are tender.

3 Mix the flour and sherry to a smooth paste. Stir the mixture into the vegetables with the cooking juices from the pigeon and the stock. Cook, covered, for 10 minutes or until boiling, stirring halfway through cooking. Arrange the pigeons in the vegetables, breast side down.

4 Reduce power to Defrost (30%) and cook, covered, for 40 minutes or until the birds are tender. Baste the pigeons halfway through cooking.

5 Meanwhile, towards the end of the cooking time, use a frying pan on the conventional hob to fry the four pieces of bread.

6 Drain the sauce from the vegetables. Arrange the fried bread on the base of a serving dish and place a pigeon on each piece. Cover each pigeon with vegetables and garnish the dish with watercress.

Freezing: Not suitable.

BLANQUETTE OF RABBIT
For 4

More hot chicken stock can be used instead of wine. If frozen rabbit joints are used, they must be thawed out first to ensure the meat is thoroughly cooked. Farmed rabbit is better than wild rabbit for this – because of the speed of microwave cooking, wild rabbit is sometimes difficult to cook until tender in the microwave. This dish is suitable for freezing.

PREPARATION: About 10 minutes
COOKING: About 1 hour 3 minutes
SETTING: Full power (100%) and
    Defrost (30%)

4 rabbit joints, 900 g/2 lb total weight
1 medium onion, peeled and chopped
½ red pepper, seeds removed, finely diced
1 garlic clove, crushed
A pinch of nutmeg
A pinch of mace
25 g/1 oz butter or margarine
25 g/1 oz plain flour
120 ml/4 fl oz milk
150 ml/¼ pint dry white wine
300 ml/½ pint hot chicken stock
Salt and pepper to taste
125 g/4 oz button mushrooms, finely sliced

1 Place the rabbit joints around a large bowl with the thin ends to the centre of the bowl. Cook, covered, on Full power for 10 minutes or until the rabbit is heated through and starting to cook. Rearrange the joints halfway through cooking. Lift the joints from the bowl and set aside, covered.
2 Stir the onion, red pepper, garlic, nutmeg, mace and butter or margarine into the cooking juices in the bowl, then cook, covered, on Full power for 6 minutes or until tender, stirring halfway through cooking.
3 Stir in the flour. Gradually add the milk, white wine, stock, and salt and pepper to taste. Cook, covered, on Full power for 4 minutes or until thickened, stirring halfway through cooking.
4 Prick the joints and arrange them in the sauce, flesh side down. Cook, covered, on Full power for 8 minutes or until the rabbit is heated through.
5 Reduce power to Defrost (30%). Cook, covered, for 15 minutes. Rearrange the joints, add the mushrooms and cook, covered, for a further 20 minutes or until the rabbit is tender.

Freezing: Make sure the rabbit joints are covered by the sauce. Use within 6 months.

Thawing: Full power (100%). Use a large bowl. Cook, covered, for 25 minutes or until the liquid is boiling and the rabbit is completely heated through, remembering to break it up and rearrange it gently – after 15 minutes of heating time.

Chapter 7
Main Course Meats

ROASTING MEAT

The conventional oven makes a good partner for the microwave when it comes to cooking larger joints of meat in double-quick time. Start the cooking in the microwave, then transfer the meat to a conventional oven for a short time for it to crisp and brown as it finishes cooking. After microwaving, allow about 15 to 20 minutes in a conventional oven preheated to Gas 4, 350°F, 180°C, but check that the meat from the microwave is in a suitably ovenproof container before transferring it to the conventional oven.

ROASTING TIMES FOR BEEF
Use the following table to calculate the microwave cooking times, depending on how well done you like your meat:

Rare:
5 mins to the 450 g/1 lb

Medium-rare:
6 to 7 mins to the 450 g/1 lb

Well-done:
8 to 9 mins to the 450 g/1 lb

RIB OF BEEF
Enough for 4 to 6

Unless you are planning to eat the meat cold, it would be better not to freeze the whole joint 'in the piece'. Thawing it in the microwave will dry it out and alter the succulent texture. The best way to freeze roast meat is in slices, with gravy, then remember to reheat it thoroughly in the gravy before serving.

PREPARATION: About 10 minutes
COOKING: About 31 minutes, plus 5 minutes standing time
SETTING: Full power (100%) and a conventional oven

A rib of beef, weighing about 1.25 kg/2¾ lb in total

1 Place the beef on a trivet, or on an upturned plate set in a shallow microproof dish. Cook, uncovered, on Full power for 16 minutes, turning the meat over halfway through cooking. Pour off any cooking juices for the gravy.
2 Preheat the conventional oven to Gas 4, 350°F, 180°C, and transfer the meat to an ovenproof dish, if necessary. Cook in the preheated oven for 15 minutes, during which time the joint will brown and the outside turn crisp as it finishes cooking.
3 Leave to stand on a warm serving dish for 5 minutes for the juices to redistribute themselves throughout the meat before carving.
Freezing: Slice the meat and arrange it in a shallow dish. Pour over 300 ml/½ pint of stock or gravy. Use within 6 months.
Thawing: Full power (100%). Use a shallow dish. Cook, covered, for 10 minutes, or until the meat is thoroughly heated through. Separate the slices after 4 minutes and rearrange them after 7 minutes. Smaller quantities will take only a few minutes – check the thawing and reheating after every minute.

TRADITIONAL ROAST TOPSIDE OF BEEF
(Medium-rare)
For 6 to 8 people

PREPARATION: About 5 minutes
COOKING: About 48 minutes, plus 5 minutes standing time
SETTING: Full power (100%) and a conventional oven

A 1.8 kg/4 lb topside joint of beef

1 Place the meat on a trivet, or on an upturned plate set in a shallow microproof dish. Cook, uncovered, on

Full power for 28 minutes, turning the meat over halfway through cooking. Pour off any juices for making gravy.

2 Preheat the conventional oven to Gas 4, 350°F, 180°C and transfer the meat to an ovenproof dish, if necessary. Cook in the preheated oven for 20 minutes, turning the meat over once, halfway through the cooking time.

3 Leave to stand on a warm serving dish for 5 minutes before carving, to allow the juices to redistribute themselves throughout the meat.

Freezing: Slice the meat before freezing and arrange it in a shallow dish. Pour over 300 ml/½ pint of stock or gravy. (This helps prevent the meat from drying out.) Use within 6 months.

Thawing: Full power (100%). Place in a shallow dish. Cook, covered, for 12 minutes or until the meat is completely heated through. Separate the slices after 4 minutes and rearrange them after 8 minutes. Smaller quantities take less time, so check after a few minutes, and continue checking after every minute.

STIR-FRY BEEF
For 4

This is an easy recipe for a speedy main course which takes very little cooking time. It is best freshly made – to retain the crisp 'bite' of the vegetables and meat. If frozen, this texture is lost during thawing.

PREPARATION: About 15 minutes
COOKING: About 9 minutes, plus 4
    minutes standing time
SETTING: Full power (100%)

1 tablespoon olive oil or
    vegetable oil
1 bunch spring onions, trimmed
    and roughly chopped
125 g/4 oz carrot, trimmed,
    peeled and coarsely grated

2 garlic cloves, crushed
575 g/1¼ lb fillet steak, cut into
    5 by 1-cm/3 by ½-inch strips
125 g/4 oz button mushrooms,
    finely sliced
15 g/½ oz cornflour
1 tablespoon water
60 ml/2 fl oz dry sherry
180 ml/6 fl oz hot beef stock
2 tablespoons soy sauce
Salt and pepper to taste
50 g/2 oz unsalted cashew nuts

1 Place the oil, onions, carrot and garlic in a large bowl. Cook, covered, for 3 minutes, until partially softened, stirring halfway through cooking.

2 Stir in the steak and mushrooms. Cook, covered, for 3 minutes.

3 Mix the cornflour to a smooth paste with the water and sherry. Stir into the steak mixture with the hot stock, soy sauce, salt and pepper and cashew nuts. Cover and cook for 3 minutes, or until thickened. If the meat is not cooked to the required degree, stand, covered, for 4 minutes before serving.

Freezing: Not suitable.

DEVILLED STEAK
For 4

This can also be made with lamb or pork fillet. It is suitable for freezing.

PREPARATION: About 20 minutes
COOKING: About 52 minutes
SETTING: Full power (100%) and
    Defrost (30%)

1 bunch spring onions, trimmed
    and left whole
½ red pepper, seeds removed,
    cut into thin strips
½ yellow pepper, seeds removed,
    cut into thin strips
125 g/4 oz carrot, peeled and cut
    into matchsticks
2 tablespoons olive oil or
    vegetable oil

1 level teaspoon dried mixed
herbs
575 g/1¼ lb braising steak, well
beaten and cut into 7.5 by
1-cm/3 by ½-inch strips
125 g/4 oz mushrooms, thinly
sliced
25 g/1 oz demerara sugar
1 tablespoon Worcestershire
sauce
1 tablespoon soy sauce
1 rounded tablespoon tomato
sauce
150 ml/¼ pint dry red wine
150 ml/¼ pint hot beef stock
Salt and pepper to taste
½ level teaspoon chilli powder
1 level tablespoon cornflour
3 tablespoons water

1 Put the onions, peppers, carrot, oil
and herbs into a large bowl. Cook,
covered, for 8 minutes or until the
vegetables are tender. Stir in the meat
and cook, covered, for 6 minutes or
until partially cooked, stirring halfway
through cooking.
2 Stir in the mushrooms, sugar,
Worcestershire sauce, soy sauce,
tomato sauce, wine, salt and
pepper and chilli powder. Cook,
covered, for 5 minutes or until
boiling.
3 Stir, then reduce power to Defrost
(30%). Cook for 30 minutes or until
the meat is tender.
4 Transfer the meat and vegetables
to a warm serving dish with a slotted
spoon. Keep warm.
5 Blend the cornflour with the water,
then stir it into the hot sauce.
Increase to Full power (100%), and
cook, uncovered, for 3 minutes or
until thickened, stirring every minute.
Pour the sauce over the meat.

Freezing: Use within 6 months.

Thawing: Full power (100%). Use a
large bowl. Cook, uncovered, for 18
minutes or until the sauce is boiling
and the steak is completely heated
through. Break up and stir after 10
and 12 minutes.

BEEF COBBLER
For 4

*A good beef stew with an old-fashioned
scone topping. The stew can be frozen
and the scones can be made during the
thawing and reheating process. If frozen
with the meat, they go soggy during
thawing.*

PREPARATION: About 20 minutes
COOKING: About 1 hour 11 minutes
SETTING: Full power (100%),
Defrost (30%) and a conventional
oven

1 medium onion, peeled and
finely chopped
125 g/4 oz carrots, peeled and
thinly sliced
1 courgette, trimmed and thinly
sliced
½ yellow pepper, seeds removed,
finely diced
25 g/1 oz butter or margarine,
cut into pieces
575 g/1¼ lb braising steak, cut
into 1-cm/½-inch cubes
1 level teaspoon mixed dried
herbs
25 g/1 oz plain flour
600 ml/1 pint hot beef stock
Salt and pepper to taste
½ teaspoon gravy browning

SCONE TOPPING
225 g/8 oz self-raising flour
50 g/2 oz margarine
A pinch of salt
3 tablespoons milk
3 tablespoons water
Half an egg, lightly beaten

1 Place the onion, carrots, courgette,
pepper and butter or margarine into
a large bowl. Cook, covered, for 6
minutes or until the vegetables are
partially cooked, stirring halfway
through cooking.
2 Stir in the steak and cook, covered,
for 5 minutes to seal the meat.

3 Stir in the herbs, flour, hot stock, salt and pepper to taste and the gravy browning. Cook, covered, for 5 minutes or until thickened.

4 Stir, reduce to Defrost (30%) and cook, covered, for 40 minutes or until the meat is tender.

5 Meanwhile, make the scone topping. Rub together the flour and margarine until the mixture resembles fine breadcrumbs. Add a pinch of salt. Stir in the milk and water to bind, then roll out the pastry to 1 cm/½ inch thick and cut into 8, 5-cm/2-inch rounds.

6 When the stew is cooked, spoon it into an ovenproof casserole. Arrange the scones on top of the mixture and brush each with beaten egg. Bake in a preheated hot oven Gas 8, 450°F/230°C for 15 minutes, or until the scones are risen and golden brown.

Freezing: Freeze after step 4. Use within 6 months.

Thawing: Full power (100%). Use a large bowl. Cook, covered, for 20 minutes or until the liquid is boiling and the meat is completely heated through. Break up with a fork after 10 minutes, and stir after 15 minutes. Continue as given in steps 5 and 6.

CASSEROLE OF BEEF WITH DUMPLINGS
For 4

A traditional winter-warming main course; for a change, add a teaspoon of mixed dried herbs to the dumpling mixture after the rubbing-in stage. A suitable dish for freezing.

PREPARATION: About 20 minutes, plus 4 to 6 hours marinating time
COOKING: About 1 hour 6 minutes
SETTING: Full power (100%) and Defrost (30%)

MARINADE
3 tablespoons olive or vegetable oil
3 tablespoons white wine vinegar
Salt and pepper to taste
1 level teaspoon mixed dried herbs

CASSEROLE MIXTURE
575 g/1¼ lb braising beef, cut into 1-cm/½-inch cubes
1 leek, trimmed and thinly sliced
125 g/4 oz carrots, peeled and thinly sliced
½ red pepper, seeds removed, finely diced
25 g/1 oz button mushrooms, thinly sliced
2 rounded tablespoons tomato purée
25 g/1 oz plain flour
600 ml/1 pint hot beef stock

DUMPLINGS
75 g/3 oz shredded suet
175 g/6 oz self-raising flour
A pinch of salt
8 tablespoons cold water

1 Mix together the oil, vinegar, salt and pepper to taste and herbs. Put the meat into a medium bowl, mix in the marinade and leave for 4 to 6 hours, stirring several times during standing. Drain, and discard the marinade.

2 Place the leek, carrot, red pepper, mushrooms and tomato purée in a large bowl. Cook, covered, for 8 minutes or until tender, stirring halfway through cooking.

3 Stir in the flour, then the meat; gradually stir in the hot stock. Cook, covered, for 10 minutes or until boiling vigorously, stirring halfway through cooking.

4 Stir again, cover, then reduce power to Defrost (30%). Cook for 40 minutes, or until the meat is tender.

5 Meanwhile, make the dumplings. Mix together the suet, flour and salt.

Add enough water to bind the mixture, then make into 12 small balls. Set aside until the meat is cooked.
6 Add the dumplings to the stew and push each one under the liquid to moisten them. Increase power to Full (100%) and cook, covered, for 8 minutes or until the dumplings are cooked.

Freezing: Use within 1 month.

Thawing: Full power (100%). Use a large bowl. Cook, covered, for 20 minutes or until the liquid is boiling and the meat is completely heated through. Gently break up with a fork after 10 minutes and stir after 15 minutes. Be careful not to damage dumplings.

CURRIED BEEF
For 4

A mild curry, particularly suitable for freezing. For a stronger flavour, add more curry powder to taste. Serve with rice.

PREPARATION: About 15 minutes
COOKING: About 1 hour 6 minutes
SETTING: Full power (100%) and
  Defrost (30%)

2 large onions, peeled and
  coarsely chopped
2 garlic cloves, crushed
1 level tablespoon mild curry
  powder
25 g/1 oz butter or margarine
575 g/1¼ lb braising steak, cut
  into 1-cm/½-inch cubes
25 g/1 oz plain flour
397 g/14 oz can of tomatoes,
  with juice
2 rounded tablespoons tomato
  purée
150 ml/¼ pint hot beef stock
1 tablespoon lemon juice
1 small dessert apple, peeled,
  cored and coarsely diced
¼ level teaspoon grated nutmeg

¼ level teaspoon coriander
  powder
½ level teaspoon chilli powder
Salt and pepper to taste

1 Put the onions, garlic, curry powder and butter or margarine in a large bowl. Cook, covered, on Full power for 10 minutes or until tender, stirring halfway through cooking.
2 Stir in the meat. Cook, covered, for 6 minutes to seal the meat, stirring halfway through cooking.
3 Stir in the flour. Add the tomatoes with their juice, tomato purée, hot stock, lemon juice, apple, nutmeg, coriander, chilli powder, and salt and pepper. Cook, covered, for 20 minutes to thicken and give time for the flavours to develop, stirring after 5 minutes.
4 Stir, reduce power to Defrost (30%), and cook, covered, for 30 minutes or until the meat is tender and the flavours have fully developed.

Freezing: Use within 6 months.

Thawing: Full power (100%). Use a large bowl. Cook, covered, for 20 minutes or until the liquid is boiling and the meat is completely heated through. Break up and stir after 10 and 15 minutes.

MINCED BEEF WITH NUT CRUMBLE
For 4

This is a novel way to serve the ever popular minced beef. The meat can be frozen, and the topping can be made while the meat is thawing and reheated, so the topping doesn't lose its crisp texture during thawing.

PREPARATION: About 15 minutes
COOKING: About 14 minutes,
  excluding frying time
SETTING: Full power (100%) and
  conventional hob

1 large onion, peeled and finely
   chopped
1 level teaspoon dried mixed
   herbs or 2 teaspoons chopped
   fresh herbs
2 rounded tablespoons tomato
   purée
Salt and pepper to taste
1 rounded tablespoon sweet
   pickle
450 g/1 lb minced beef

TOPPING
25 g/1 oz porridge oats
25 g/1 oz soft white or brown
   breadcrumbs
50 g/2 oz chopped walnuts
25 to 50 g/1 to 2 oz butter or
   margarine
$\frac{1}{2}$ to 1 tablespoon oil

1 Put the onion in a large bowl with
the herbs. Cook, covered, for 6
minutes or until the onion is tender,
stirring halfway through cooking.
2 Stir in the tomato purée, salt and
pepper, the pickle, and the minced
beef. Cook, covered, for 8 minutes or
until the meat is cooked, stirring
halfway through cooking.
3 While the meat is cooking, make
the topping. Mix together the oats,
breadcrumbs and walnuts. Melt the
butter or margarine and oil in a
conventional frying pan. Sprinkle in
the topping mixture and fry until
golden-brown, stirring the mixture all
the time to prevent it burning.
4 Spoon the meat into a warm
casserole dish and sprinkle the
topping over.

Freezing: Freeze after step 2. Use
within 3 months.

Thawing: Full power (100%). Place
in a large bowl. Cook, covered, for 10
minutes or until the meat is
completely heated through, breaking
it up and stirring it halfway through
cooking. While thawing and heating
the meat, fry the topping as given in
step 3 and continue the recipe as
above.

SPICY MEATBALLS IN CARROT AND TOMATO SAUCE
For 4

*Delicious as a main course, or hot buffet
party dish with each meatball pierced
by a cocktail stick. Suitable for
freezing.*

PREPARATION: About 15 minutes
COOKING: About 18 minutes
SETTING: Full power (100%)

SAUCE
125 g/4 oz carrot, peeled and
   finely grated
1 medium onion, peeled and
   finely chopped
1 tablespoon malt vinegar
1 rounded tablespoon tomato
   purée
2 garlic cloves, crushed
2 tablespoons soy sauce
1 tablespoon Worcestershire
   sauce
25 g/1 oz plain flour
225 g/8 oz can of tomatoes, with
   juice
150 ml/$\frac{1}{4}$ pint hot beef stock
Salt and pepper to taste

MEAT BALLS
325 g/12 oz minced beef
1 medium onion, peeled and
   minced or grated
50 g/2 oz porridge oats
2 tablespoons soy sauce
Salt and pepper to taste
1 (size 1) egg, lightly beaten
Chopped fresh parsley or
   chives, to garnish

1 For the sauce: Put the carrot,
onion, vinegar, tomato purée, garlic,
soy sauce and Worcestershire sauce in
a large bowl. Cook, covered, for 5
minutes or until the vegetables are
tender.
2 Stir in the flour, then gradually
blend in the tomatoes and juice, hot

89

stock and salt and pepper to taste. Cook, uncovered, for 3 minutes or until thickened, stirring every minute. Put through a liquidiser or food processor until smooth. Set aside.

3 Make the meatballs: Mix together the beef, onion, oats, soy sauce, and salt and pepper to taste. Bind the mixture together with the egg. Using floured hands, roll into 16 meatballs.

4 Arrange these in a shallow dish. Cook, covered, for 6 minutes or until cooked throughout, rearranging them after 4 minutes.

5 Pour the sauce over the meatballs and cook, uncovered, for 4 minutes or until the sauce is boiling and the meatballs are completely heated through. Garnish with chopped parsley or chives.

Freezing: Freeze before garnishing. Use within 3 months.

Thawing: Full power (100%). Use a large bowl. Cook, covered, for 20 minutes or until the liquid is boiling and the meatballs are completely heated through. Gently break up and rearrange after 10 and 15 minutes.

MINT-STUFFED LEG OF LAMB

For 6 to 8

Ask the butcher to bone the joint to save your time. Freezing the joint is not recommended as the meat needs to be completely heated through if served hot and when this is done during thawing, the meat dries out. However, the meat can be successfully frozen in slices, with gravy.

PREPARATION: About 20 minutes, plus 5 minutes standing time
COOKING: About 48 minutes
SETTING: Full power (100%) and a conventional oven

1 tablespoon white wine vinegar
1 tablespoon oil
2 kg 25 g/4½ lb leg lamb (weight before boning), boned

STUFFING
50 g/2 oz fresh white breadcrumbs
2 teaspoons mint sauce
1 small dessert apple, peeled, cored and finely chopped
Salt and pepper to taste
1 egg (size 2), lightly beaten

1 Mix the vinegar and oil together and brush the outside and inside of the meat with the mixture.

2 Now make the stuffing: Mix together the breadcrumbs, mint sauce, apple, salt and pepper and bind with the beaten egg.

3 Stuff the lamb and tie it up with string. Weigh the meat and calculate the cooking time by allowing 7 minutes to the 450 g/1 lb.

4 Place the joint on a trivet, or on an upturned plate set in a shallow microproof dish. Cook, uncovered, on Full power for the calculated time, turning the meat over halfway through the cooking time. Pour off any juices and use to make the gravy.

5 Preheat the conventional oven to Gas 4, 350°F, 180°C and transfer the meat to an ovenproof dish, if necessary. Cook for 20 minutes, turning the meat over halfway through roasting.

6 Leave the meat to stand on a warm serving dish for 5 minutes before carving.

Freezing: Slice the meat and arrange it in a shallow dish. Pour over the 300 ml/½ pint of stock or gravy. Use within 6 months.

Thawing: Full power (100%). Place the meat in a shallow dish and cook, covered, for 16 minutes or until the meat is completely heated throughout. Separate the slices after 6 minutes and rearrange them after 10 minutes. Smaller quantities will take only a few minutes to thaw and reheat.

LAMB WITH AUBERGINE
For 4

To avoid a bitter taste from the aubergine, it is important to follow the instructions in step 1. Serve with thick pieces of French bread to mop up the delicious juices. If you prefer to thicken the sauce, blend 25 g/1 oz cornflour with 4 tablespoons water and stir this into the mixture after step 3. The recipe is suitable for freezing.

PREPARATION: About 10 minutes, plus 20 minutes standing time for the aubergine
COOKING: About 35 minutes
SETTING: Full power (100%)

1 aubergine, 325 g/12 oz total weight, trimmed and thinly sliced
Salt
1 tablespoon olive oil or vegetable oil
1 medium onion, peeled and finely chopped
1 large carrot, peeled, trimmed and thinly sliced
1 level teaspoon dried mixed herbs
½ level teaspoon dried chopped mint
8 lamb chops, 900 g/2 lb total weight
400 g/14 oz can of tomatoes with juice, chopped
300 ml/½ pint hot beef stock
Salt and pepper to taste

1 Sprinkle the aubergine slices with salt and leave to stand for 20 minutes. Rinse well in cold water and pat dry.
2 Put the oil in a large bowl with the onion, carrot, herbs and mint. Cook, covered, for 8 minutes or until the vegetables are tender, stirring halfway through cooking.
3 Arrange the chops around the sides and base of the bowl. Cook, covered, for 7 minutes or until heated through, rearranging them halfway through cooking. Add the tomatoes and juice, hot stock and salt and pepper to taste.
4 Arrange the aubergine slices on top. Cook, covered, for 20 minutes or until the chops are tender, stirring halfway through cooking.
Freezing: Use within 6 months.
Thawing: Full power (100%). Use a large bowl and cook, covered, for 30 minutes or until the liquid is boiling and the chops are completely heated through. Gently break up after 10 minutes and rearrange after 15 minutes.

EASTERN-STYLE LAMB
For 4

A lightly spiced, pleasant way of serving lamb in a different style. It is not suitable for freezing as the sauce thickens up and looks unpalatable during thawing.

PREPARATION: About 15 minutes, plus 8 to 12 hours refrigeration.
COOKING: About 33 minutes
SETTING: Full power (100%) and Defrost (30%)

4 tablespoons olive oil or vegetable oil
1 large onion, peeled and finely chopped
2 garlic cloves, peeled and finely chopped
1 level teaspoon cumin powder
½ level teaspoon ground black pepper
1 level teaspoon salt
A 5-cm/2-inch piece of dried ginger, beaten with a mallet to bruise
325 g/12 oz natural yogurt
675 g/1½ lb lean lamb, cut into 1-cm/½-inch cubes
20 g/¾ oz cornflour
3 tablespoons water

2 tablespoons lemon juice
½ teaspoon dried fenugreek
  leaves
1 to 2 tablespoons chopped
  fresh parsley, to garnish

1 Combine the oil, onion, garlic, cumin powder, black pepper, salt and ginger in a large bowl and mix well. Stir in the yogurt and lamb. Cover the bowl and refrigerate for 8 to 12 hours, stirring occasionally.
2 Cook, covered, on Full power for 15 minutes to seal and heat the meat through, stirring halfway through cooking. Stir and reduce power to Defrost (30%). Cook, covered, for 15 minutes or until the meat is tender.
3 In a small bowl, blend the cornflour with the water and lemon juice to make a smooth paste. Remove the ginger from the lamb and discard it; add the fenugreek and stir in the cornflour mixture. Increase to Full power (100%). Cook, uncovered, for 3 minutes or until thickened, stirring every minute.
4 Spoon on to a warm serving dish and sprinkle with parsley to garnish.
Freezing: Not suitable.

LAMB WITH FRESH CHERRIES
For 4

Only use red or black cherries as others tend to discolour when frozen. For a more economical version, substitute chicken or lamb stock for the wine. This recipe is suitable for freezing.

PREPARATION: About 15 minutes
COOKING: About 45 minutes
SETTING: Full power (100%) and
  Defrost (30%)

25 g/1 oz butter or margarine
**800 g/1¾ lb lamb fillet, cut into
  2.5-cm/1-inch cubes**

1 level teaspoon dried oregano
25 g/1 oz plain flour
60 ml/2 fl oz dry white wine
90 ml/3 fl oz milk
150 ml/¼ pint hot lamb or
  chicken stock
Salt and pepper to taste
325 g/12 oz fresh cherries, stalks
  and stones removed, cut in
  half

1 Put the butter or margarine, lamb and oregano in a large bowl. Cook, covered, on Full power for 10 minutes to seal the meat, stirring halfway through cooking.
2 Stir in the flour and then the wine, milk, stock, salt and pepper. Cook, covered, for 15 minutes until the sauce is boiling and the meat is completely heated through, stirring halfway through cooking.
3 Stir in the halved cherries. Reduce power to Defrost (30%) and cook for 20 minutes or until the meat is tender, stirring halfway through cooking.

Freezing: Use within 6 months.

Thawing: Full power (100%). Use a large bowl. Cook, covered, for 20 minutes or until the liquid is boiling and the meat is completely heated through. Break up and stir after 10 and 15 minutes.

LAMB STEW WITH VEGETABLES AND HERBS
For 4

An economical family meal, this makes a filling main course when served with boiled potatoes. It can be frozen.

PREPARATION: About 15 minutes
COOKING: About 55 minutes
SETTING: Full power (100%) and
  Defrost (30%)

1 large carrot, peeled and thinly
  sliced
1 courgette, trimmed and thinly
  sliced
1 small red pepper, seeds
  removed, finely diced
1 medium onion, peeled and
  roughly chopped
2 sticks celery, trimmed and
  roughly chopped
$\frac{1}{4}$ level teaspoon dried rosemary
$\frac{1}{4}$ level teaspoon dried parsley
$\frac{1}{4}$ level teaspoon dried sage
25 g/1 oz butter or margarine
675 g/1$\frac{1}{2}$ lb neck fillet lamb, cut
  into 2.5-cm/1-inch cubes
25 g/1 oz plain flour
300 ml/$\frac{1}{2}$ pint hot lamb or chicken
  stock
50 g/2 oz button mushrooms,
  wiped
Salt and pepper to taste

1 Put the carrot, courgette, red
pepper, onion, celery, rosemary,
parsley, sage and butter or margarine
in a large bowl. Cook, covered, on
Full power for 9 minutes or until the
vegetables are tender, stirring halfway
through cooking.
2 Stir in the meat and cook, covered,
for 6 minutes or until it is heated
through, stirring halfway through
cooking.
3 Stir in the flour and blend in the
stock. Stir in the mushrooms and salt
and pepper to taste. Cook, covered,
for 25 minutes stirring after 10
minutes.
4 Reduce power to Defrost (30%), and
cook, covered, for 15 minutes or until
the meat is tender. Spoon into a warm
serving dish.

Freezing: Use within 6 months.

Thawing: Full power (100%). Use a
large bowl. Cook, covered, for 20
minutes or until the liquid is boiling
and the meat is completely heated
through. Break up and stir after 10
and 15 minutes.

94

DEVILLED LAMBS KIDNEYS
For 4

*A spicy dish that is suitable for
freezing.*

PREPARATION: About 15 minutes
COOKING: About 17 minutes
SETTING: Full power (100%)

3 tablespoons olive oil or
  vegetable oil
1 garlic clove, crushed
1 red pepper, seeds removed,
  finely diced
1 large onion, peeled and finely
  chopped
8 lambs kidneys, halved and
  cored
25 g/1 oz plain flour
225 g/8 oz can of tomatoes, with
  juice
150 ml/$\frac{1}{4}$ pint hot lamb or
  chicken stock
Salt and pepper to taste
1 tablespoon Worcestershire
  sauce
A dash of Tabasco sauce
1 tablespoon malt vinegar
2 rounded tablespoons tomato
  purée
$\frac{1}{4}$ level teaspoon dry English
  mustard

1 Put the oil, garlic, red pepper and
onion in a large bowl. Cook, covered,
for 6 minutes or until the vegetables
are tender, stirring halfway through
cooking. Stir in the kidneys and cook,
covered, for 3 minutes or until they
are partially cooked.
2 Stir in the flour. Gradually stir in
the tomatoes, stock, salt, pepper,
Worcestershire sauce, Tabasco sauce,
malt vinegar, tomato purée and
mustard. Cook, covered, for 8 minutes
or until the kidneys are tender,
stirring halfway through cooking. Do
not overcook, or the kidneys will
toughen.
Freezing: Use within 3 months.

Thawing: Full power (100%). Use a large bowl. Cook, covered, for 20 minutes or until the liquid is boiling and the kidneys are completely heated through. Break up after 10 and 15 minutes.

LAMBS LIVER IN RED WINE
For 4

Frozen liver may be used, but it must be thawed first to ensure thorough cooking. For an economical recipe, use hot lamb stock instead of the wine. It is suitable for freezing.

PREPARATION: About 10 minutes
COOKING: About 16 minutes, plus 5
   minutes standing time
SETTING: Full power (100%)

1 garlic clove, crushed
25 g/1 oz butter or margarine
4 rashers streaky bacon, rinds
   removed, chopped
1 medium onion, peeled and
   finely chopped
$\frac{1}{2}$ green pepper, seeds removed,
   finely diced
25 g/1 oz plain flour
125 ml/$\frac{1}{4}$ pint red wine
125 ml/$\frac{1}{4}$ pint hot lamb stock
225 g/8 oz tomatoes, skinned
   and chopped
1 rounded tablespoon tomato
   purée
1 level teaspoon dried mixed
   herbs
Salt and pepper to taste
450 g/1 lb lambs liver, skinned
   and finely sliced

1 Place the garlic, butter or margarine, bacon, onion and green pepper in a large bowl. Cook, covered, for 6 minutes or until the vegetables are tender, stirring halfway through cooking.

2 Stir the flour into the vegetables, stir in the wine, stock, tomatoes, the purée, herbs, salt, pepper and liver.
3 Cook, covered, for 10 minutes or until the liver is tender, stirring halfway through cooking. Stand, covered, for 5 minutes before serving.

Freezing: Use within 3 months.

Thawing: Full power (100%). Use a large bowl. Cook, covered, for 30 minutes or until the liquid is boiling and the liver is completely heated through. Break up after 7 minutes, stir and rearrange after 11 minutes and again after 20 minutes.

FRICASSEE OF LAMBS SWEETBREADS
For 4 or 5

This will serve 8 for a starter, and makes a delicious introduction to sweetbreads for anyone who has not tried them before. Serve with a selection of vegetables. The dish is suitable for freezing.

PREPARATION: About 30 minutes,
   plus soaking and standing time,
   about 2 hours 10 minutes
COOKING: About 20 minutes
SETTING: Full power (100%)

900 g/2 lb fresh or thawed lambs
   sweetbreads
About 1.2 litres/2 pints
   lukewarm water, for soaking
2 tablespoons white wine
   vinegar
1.2 litres/2 pints boiling water
50 g/2 oz butter
50 g/2 oz plain flour
150 ml/$\frac{1}{4}$ pint milk
150 ml/$\frac{1}{4}$ pint hot chicken stock
Salt and pepper to taste
125 g/4 oz button mushrooms,
   finely sliced

A good pinch of grated nutmeg
Finely grated rind of 1 lemon
2 tablespoons double cream
Sprigs of parsley and slices of
    lemon, to garnish

1 Cover the sweetbreads in lukewarm
water to which 1 tablespoon vinegar
has been added. Soak for 1 hour.
Renew the water/vinegar mixture and
soak for a further 1 hour.
2 Remove the fat and skin from the
sweetbreads and place in a medium
bowl. Pour over the boiling water,
bring it back to the boil, then cook,
uncovered, for 8 minutes or until the
sweetbreads are cooked. They should
look opaque, with no traces of pink.
3 Drain the sweetbreads and plunge
into cold water. Stand for 10 minutes.
Drain and set aside.
4 Put the butter into a large bowl.
Cook, uncovered, for 1 minute or

until melted. Stir in the flour, then
the milk, hot stock and salt and
pepper to taste. Cook, uncovered, for
3 minutes or until thickened, stirring
every minute.
5 Stir in the mushrooms, nutmeg,
lemon rind and sweetbreads. Cook,
covered, for 8 minutes or until the
mushrooms are tender, stirring
halfway through cooking.
6 Stir in the cream. Transfer the
fricassée on to a warm serving dish
and garnish with sprigs of parsley and
slices of lemon.

Freezing: Freeze before garnishing.
Use within 1 month.

Thawing: Full power (100%). Use a
medium bowl. Cook, covered, for 12
minutes or until the sauce is boiling
and the sweetbreads are heated
through. Break up after 4 minutes and
stir after 9 minutes.

ROAST PORK WITH SAGE
For 4 to 6

Unless the meat is to be eaten cold and thawed at room temperature, it is best not to freeze the whole joint. The heat generated during thawing and reheating results in the meat drying out. However, the meat can be frozen in slices with gravy.

PREPARATION: About 5 minutes
COOKING: About 44 minutes, plus 5
   minutes standing time
SETTING: Full power (100%) and a
   conventional oven

About 1 tablespoon oil
1 tablespoon dried chopped
   sage, or 2 tablespoons
   chopped fresh sage
Salt
1.3 kg/3 lb leg of pork

1 Brush oil over the inside of a roasting bag. Sprinkle the sage inside to stick lightly to the oil.
2 Sprinkle salt over the pork skin and rub it well in. This will help towards a crispy skin at the end of cooking. Place the pork in the bag and tie the bag with a non-metallic tie. Pierce the bag on both sides.
3 Place the meat in a shallow container and cook for 24 minutes, turning over halfway through cooking.
4 Remove the bag, retaining the cooking juices for gravy. Transfer the meat into a conventional oven preheated to Gas 4, 350°F, 180°C. (Check that the roasting container is ovenproof.) Roast the meat for 20 minutes, turning it over halfway through cooking.
5 Let the meat stand for 5 minutes on a warm serving dish before carving.
Freezing: Slice the meat and arrange it in a shallow dish. Pour over 300

ml/½ pint stock or gravy. Use within 3 months.
Thawing: Full power (100%). Use a shallow dish. Cook, covered, for 12 minutes or until the meat is heated through. Separate the slices after 4 minutes and rearrange them after 8 minutes. Smaller quantities will take only a few minutes.

PORK WITH CREAM SAUCE AND ALMONDS
For 4

This makes a delicious main course for a special dinner. It is not suitable for freezing as the sauce separates and loses its consistency during thawing.

PREPARATION: About 10 minutes
COOKING: About 37½ minutes
SETTING: Full power (100%)

1 large onion, peeled and
   roughly chopped
2 sticks celery, roughly chopped
25 g/1 oz butter or margarine
300 ml/½ pint hot chicken stock
Salt and pepper to taste
900 g/2 lb prime cut leg of pork,
   thinly sliced, cut into 10-cm/
   4-inch strips
20 g/¾ oz cornflour
120 ml/4 fl oz double or
   whipping cream
75 g/3 oz toasted split almonds

1 Place the onion, celery and butter or margarine in a large bowl. Cook, covered, for 8 minutes or until tender.
2 Put this vegetable mixture with the hot stock through a liquidiser or blender until smooth. Season to taste with salt and pepper and set aside.
3 Put the pork into the large bowl and cook, covered, for 6 minutes or until the meat is sealed and partially cooked. Separate and stir after 4 minutes.

97

4 Stir in the vegetable sauce and cook, covered, for 20 minutes or until the pork is tender, stirring halfway through cooking.
5 Blend the cornflour with the cream and stir this into the pork. Cook, uncovered, for $3\frac{1}{2}$ minutes, stirring every minute.
6 Stir in the almonds and pour the pork into a warm serving dish.
Freezing: Not suitable.

PORK STEAKS WITH MUSTARD AND BROWN SUGAR TOPPING
For 4

This topping is also delicious on grilled beef steaks and lamb chops. The dish is not suitable for freezing as the meat toughens during thawing.

PREPARATION: About 5 minutes
COOKING: About 8 minutes, plus grilling time (optional)
SETTING: Full power (100%)

25 g/1 oz butter or margarine
2 level teaspoons wholegrain English mustard
25 g/1 oz dark brown muscovado sugar
4 pork steaks, 675 g/1$\frac{1}{2}$ lb total weight, beaten lightly
Sprigs of watercress to garnish

1 Place the butter or margarine in a small jug. Cook, uncovered, for 1 minute or until melted. Stir in the mustard and sugar.
2 Arrange the steaks in a layer in a shallow dish. Spread each steak with a teaspoon of the mustard mixture. Cook, covered, for 7 minutes or until the steaks are cooked, turning them over and rearranging them halfway through cooking. At this stage, spread each steak with the remaining mustard mixture.

3 If desired, after cooking, the steaks can be browned under a preheated conventional grill. Arrange them on a warm flameproof serving dish. Pour over a little of the sauce.
4 Garnish the dish with sprigs of watercress.
Freezing: Not suitable.

PORK CHOP CASSEROLE
For 4

This freezes well: Lamb chops can be used instead of pork chops.

PREPARATION: About 10 minutes
COOKING: About 50 minutes to 1 hour
SETTING: Full power (100%) and Defrost (30%)

1 large onion, peeled and finely chopped
1 green pepper, seeds removed, finely diced
15 g/$\frac{1}{2}$ oz plain flour
397 g/14 oz can of tomatoes, chopped, with juice
1 chicken stock cube, crumbled
2 rounded tablespoons tomato sauce
Salt and pepper to taste
4 pork chops, 675 g/1$\frac{1}{2}$ lb total weight

1 Place the onion and green pepper in a large bowl. Cook, covered, on Full power for 7 minutes.
2 Stir in the flour, then blend in the tomatoes and juice, the chicken stock cube, tomato sauce, and salt and pepper to taste. Cook, covered, for 3 minutes or until the vegetables are partially cooked.
3 Stir them, add the chops, making sure that they are covered with sauce to prevent them drying out. Cook, covered, for 10 minutes or until the sauce is boiling. Reduce power to

Defrost (30%) and cook for 30 to 40 minutes, or until the chops are tender.

4 Arrange the chops on a hot serving dish and use a straining spoon to lift out the vegetables. Divide between the chops and serve the remaining sauce separately.

Freezing: Use within 3 months.

Thawing: Full power (100%). Use a large bowl. Cook, covered, for 30 minutes or until the liquid is boiling and the meat is completely heated through. Gently separate the chops after 10 minutes, and stir and rearrange after 20 minutes.

PORK SPARE RIBS WITH CHILLI SAUCE
For 4

The spare ribs could be served with Barbecue sauce (page 118). This recipe is suitable for freezing.

PREPARATION: About 15 minutes
COOKING: About 26 minutes
SETTING: Full power (100%) and conventional grill

1 tablespoon olive oil
2 garlic cloves, crushed
1 medium onion, peeled and finely chopped
227 g/8 oz can of tomatoes, with juice
1 tablespoon lemon juice
150 ml/$\frac{1}{4}$ pint red wine
$\frac{1}{2}$ to 1 level teaspoon chilli powder
A dash of Tabasco sauce
1 tablespoon soy sauce
1 tablespoon demerara sugar
Salt and pepper to taste
800 g/1$\frac{3}{4}$ lb spare ribs
1 level tablespoon cornflour
3 tablespoons water

1 Put the oil, garlic and onion in a shallow rectangular dish. Cook,

covered, for 3 minutes or until the onions are softened. Stir in the tomatoes and juice, lemon juice, red wine, chilli powder, Tabasco sauce, soy sauce, sugar, and salt and pepper to taste.

2 Add the ribs and coat with the sauce. Cook, covered, for 20 minutes or until the meat is tender, rearranging the ribs halfway through cooking.

3 Remove the ribs and crisp under a preheated hot grill. Meanwhile, blend the cornflour and water together and stir into the hot sauce. Cook, uncovered, for 3 minutes or until thickened, stirring every minute.

4 Put the sauce through a liquidiser or food processor until smooth.

5 Arrange the ribs on a warm serving dish and pour the sauce over.

Freezing: Use within 6 months.

Thawing: Full power (100%). Use a large shallow dish. Cook, covered, for 15 minutes or until the liquid is boiling and the meat is completely heated through. Separate and rearrange the ribs halfway through cooking. Continue from step 3 above.

PORK SAUSAGE CASSEROLE
For 4

Beef or veal sausages can be used instead of pork. This dish is suitable for freezing.

PREPARATION: About 14 minutes
COOKING: About 31 minutes, excluding frying
SETTING: Full power (100%), Defrost (30%) and conventional hob

2 tablespoons cooking oil
450 g/1 lb thick pork sausages
25 g/1 oz butter or margarine
2 medium onions, peeled and finely sliced

25 g/1 oz plain flour
227 g/8 oz can of tomatoes,
  with juice, chopped
300 ml/½ pint hot beef stock
1 level teaspoon mixed dried
  herbs
1 teaspoon Worcestershire sauce
2 rounded tablespoons tomato
  purée
225 g/8 oz button mushrooms,
  thinly sliced
Salt and pepper to taste

1 Heat the oil in a frying pan and
quickly brown the sausages on a
conventional hob. Once browned,
cut each sausage into four pieces.
2 Meanwhile, place the butter or
margarine and onions in a large bowl.
Cook, covered, on Full power for 6
minutes or until the onions are tender,
stirring halfway through cooking.
3 Stir in the flour. Gradually stir in
the tomatoes and juice, then add the
stock, herbs, Worcestershire sauce,
tomato purée, mushrooms, sausages
and salt and pepper to taste. Cook,
covered, for 5 minutes or until
thickened.
4 Stir, reduce power to Defrost
(30%) and cook for 20 minutes or
until the sausages are cooked through,
stirring halfway through cooking

Freezing: Use within 3 months.

Thawing: Full power (100%). Use a
large bowl. Cook, covered, for 25
minutes or until the liquid is boiling
and the sausages are completely
heated through. Break up after 15
minutes and stir after 20 minutes.

GAMMON STEAKS WITH APPLE SAUCE
For 4

*This dish is not suitable for freezing as
the meat toughens during the thawing
process.*

PREPARATION: About 15 minutes
COOKING: About 18 minutes
SETTING: Full power (100%)

2 tablespoons orange juice
Finely grated rind of ½ an orange
1 level tablespoon caster sugar
450 g/1 lb cooking apples, peeled,
  cored and finely sliced
1 tablespoon double cream
4 gammon steaks, 900 g/2 lb total
  weight, with rind snipped
1 red-skinned apple, cored and
  finely sliced and sprigs of
  parsley, to garnish

1 Place the orange juice, rind, sugar
and apples in a large bowl. Cook,
covered, for 5 minutes or until the
apples are tender, stirring halfway
through cooking.
2 Put the apple mixture and cream
through a liquidiser or food processor
until smooth. Set aside, covered.
3 Arrange the gammon in a shallow
dish, overlapping steaks if necessary.
Cook, covered, for 10 minutes or until
the gammon is cooked, rearranging
the steaks halfway through. Drain and
arrange, overlapping, on a warm
serving dish. Keep warm.
4 Place the apple sauce in a large jug.
Cook, uncovered, for 3 minutes or
until it is completely heated through,
stirring halfway through.
Spoon some of the sauce over the
centre of each steak. Garnish with
slices of apple and sprigs of parsley
and serve the remaining sauce
separately.

Freezing: Not suitable.

SWEET AND SOUR BACON
For 4

*This recipe gives a delicious and easy
way to serve a piece of bacon. It is
suitable for freezing.*

PREPARATION: About 12 minutes
COOKING: About 23 minutes

SETTING: Full power (100%)

675 g/1½ lb bacon shoulder joint,
  rind removed, cut into 5 by
  1-cm/3 by ½-inch strips
1 red pepper, seeds removed,
  finely diced
1 green pepper, seeds removed,
  finely diced
Half a bulb of fennel, trimmed
  and roughly chopped
1 bunch of spring onions,
  trimmed and finely chopped
3 tablespoons soy sauce
1 tablespoon wine vinegar
1 tablespoon dry sherry
1 tablespoon black treacle
1 garlic clove, crushed
1 level tablespoon cornflour
4 tablespoons water
150 ml/¼ pint hot chicken stock

1 Place the bacon, red and green
peppers, fennel, onions, soy sauce,
vinegar, sherry, treacle and garlic in a
large bowl. Cook, covered, for 8
minutes or until vegetables are tender,
stirring halfway through cooking.
2 Blend the cornflour with the water
to make a smooth paste. Stir this into
the bacon mixture with the stock.
Cook, covered, for 15 minutes or until
the bacon is cooked, stirring halfway
through.
Freezing: Use within 2 months.
Thawing: Full power (100%). Place
in a large bowl. Cook, covered, for 20
minutes or until the liquid is boiling
and the bacon is completely heated
through. Break up and stir after
10 and 15 minutes.

BACON AND CABBAGE PIE
For 2 to 4

*This can be served as a main course, or
as a vegetable dish to accompany a
main course like grilled meat, roast
meat, sausages or hamburgers. It is
suitable for freezing.*

PREPARATION: About 15 minutes
COOKING: About 14 minutes, plus
  grilling time
SETTING: Full power (100%) and
  conventional grill

450 g/1 lb potatoes, peeled and
  thinly sliced
3 tablespoons water
1 large onion, peeled and
  roughly chopped
6 slices streaky bacon, rinds
  removed, chopped
1 tablespoon tomato purée
325 g/¾ lb finely shredded white
  cabbage
150 ml/¼ pint hot chicken stock
Salt and pepper to taste
25 g/1 oz Cheddar cheese, finely
  grated

1 Place the potatoes and water in a
large bowl and cook, covered, for 8
minutes or until the potatoes are
tender. Set aside, covered.
2 Put the onion, bacon and tomato
purée into a large bowl. Cook,
covered, for 6 minutes or until the
onions are cooked. Stir in the cabbage,
hot stock and salt and pepper to taste.
Cook, covered, for a further 6 minutes
or until the cabbage is tender, stirring
halfway through cooking.
3 Spoon the mixture into a deep
fireproof dish. Drain the potatoes and
arrange them over the mixture.
4 Sprinkle with the cheese and cook
under a preheated hot conventional
grill until bubbling and brown.
Freezing: Freeze after step 2. Use
within 2 months.
Thawing: Full power (100%). Place
in a large bowl. Cook, covered, for 18
minutes, stirring halfway through
cooking. Continue as from step 3.

BACON AND ONION PUDDING

For 4

If a sauce is to be served with the pudding, the Herb sauce on page 118 would make a change to gravy. The pudding must be served as soon as it is cooked. If it is allowed to cool, it will lose moisture and harden. For this reason, it is not suitable for freezing.

PREPARATION: About 10 minutes
COOKING: About 12 minutes, plus 2
   minutes standing time
SETTING: Full power (100%)

1 large onion, peeled and finely
   chopped
4 rashers streaky bacon, rinds
   removed, roughly chopped
225 g/8 oz self-raising flour
Salt and pepper to taste
125 g/4 oz shredded suet
1 (size 2) egg, lightly beaten
2 tablespoons water
Sprigs of parsley, to garnish

1 Place the onion and bacon in a medium bowl. Cook, covered, for 6 minutes or until the onion is tender, stirring halfway through cooking.
2 Stir in the flour, salt and pepper to taste, and the suet. Mix in the egg and water. Spoon into a greased 1.5 litre/2½ pint pudding basin. Cook, covered, for 6 minutes or until the mixture is soft and springy.
3 Stand, covered, for 2 minutes. Remove the cover, loosen the pudding with a knife and turn it on to a warm serving dish. Garnish with sprigs of parsley and serve at once.

Freezing: Not suitable.

Chapter 8
Rice, Pasta and Pulses

EGG RICE
For 4

This dish makes a filling main course or supper dish. It can be frozen without the egg as the egg tends to go rubbery during thawing. If the prawns have not been frozen before, then the dish can be frozen at the end of step 3.

PREPARATION: About 10 minutes
COOKING: About 19 minutes, plus
   10 minutes standing time
SETTING: Full power (100%)

1 large onion, peeled and finely
   chopped
1 garlic clove, crushed
1 tablespoon oil
325 g/12 oz long-grain rice
750 ml/1¼ pints boiling chicken
   stock
1 tablespoon soy sauce
225 g/8 oz peeled prawns
2 eggs, lightly whisked
Salt and pepper to taste

1 Place the onion, garlic and oil in a large bowl. Cook, covered, for 5 minutes or until the onion is tender.
2 Stir in the rice, boiling stock and soy sauce. Cook, covered, until the stock returns to the boil, then cook for a further 10 minutes without stirring.
3 Stir in the prawns and continue cooking for 3 minutes to warm them. Set aside, covered, for 10 minutes to finish off the cooking process.
4 Stir the eggs into the rice, adding salt and pepper to taste. Cook, uncovered, for a further 45 seconds, if necessary, to set the eggs.

Freezing: Do not add the prawns unless they have not been previously frozen. Freeze after step 2. Use within 3 months.

Thawing: Full power (100%). Use a large bowl. Cook, covered, for 12 minutes or until hot, breaking up and stirring halfway through cooking. Stir in the prawns. Cook, covered, for 3

minutes to warm the prawns – then continue from step 4.

BROWN RICE RISOTTO
For 4

This makes a filling main course or supper dish. For greater economy, cold stock can be substituted for the wine. This recipe is suitable for freezing.

PREPARATION: About 15 minutes
COOKING: About 38 minutes, plus
   10 minutes standing time
SETTING: Full power (100%)

1 teaspoon mixed dried herbs
50 g/2 oz butter or margarine
1 large onion, peeled and finely
   chopped
1 green pepper, seeds removed,
   finely diced
2 level tablespoons tomato
   purée
2 garlic cloves, crushed
1 medium carrot, peeled and
   thinly sliced
50 g/2 oz button mushrooms,
   finely sliced
2 tablespoons frozen peas
400 g/14 oz long-grain brown rice
Salt and pepper to taste
900 ml/1½ pints hot vegetable
   stock
150 ml/¼ pint dry white wine

1 Put the herbs, butter or margarine, onion, green pepper, tomato purée, garlic and carrot into a large bowl. Cook, covered, for 8 minutes or until the vegetables are tender, stirring halfway through cooking.

2 Stir in the mushrooms, peas, rice and salt and pepper to taste. Pour in the hot stock and the wine. Cover, bring back to the boil, then cook, covered, for 30 minutes. Do not stir. Set aside, still covered, to finish off the cooking process.

3 Pile the risotto into a warm serving dish.

Freezing: Use within 6 months.

Thawing: Full power (100%). Cook, covered, for 12 minutes or until the rice is completely heated through. Break it up and stir halfway through cooking.

WHOLEWHEAT BUTTERED SPAGHETTI
For 4

Wholewheat spaghetti gives additional fibre to the diet and it is delicious served with a meat or fish sauce. It can be frozen.

PREPARATION: About 5 minutes
COOKING: About 10 minutes, plus
   10 minutes standing time
SETTING: Full power (100%)

$\frac{1}{4}$ level teaspoon salt
1 tablespoon oil
1.75 litres/3 pints boiling water
225 g/8 oz wholewheat spaghetti
50 g/2 oz butter or margarine,
   cut into pieces, or 2
   tablespoons olive oil
Freshly ground black pepper

1 Place the salt, oil and the boiling water in a large bowl. Place the spaghetti in the water and cook, uncovered, for 1 minute to soften it.
2 Now push the spaghetti under the water and cook, covered, until the water comes back to the boil. Cook for 9 minutes, checking during cooking that the spaghetti is still covered with water.
3 Let it stand, covered, for 10 minutes to finish off the cooking process.
4 Drain and toss in butter, margarine or oil and sprinkle with freshly ground black pepper to serve.

Freezing: Freeze after step 3.

Thawing: Full power (100%). Use a large bowl and cook, covered, for 3 minutes to start the thawing process. Pour over 600 ml/1 pint of boiling water and continue to cook for 5 minutes or until the spaghetti is completely heated through. Gently separate the strands halfway through cooking. Continue from step 4.

MACARONI CHEESE WITH TOMATO AND OREGANO
For 4

A good variation on macaroni cheese: Suitable for freezing without the cheese topping (cheese loses texture during thawing).

PREPARATION: About 15 minutes
COOKING: About 16 minutes, plus
   8 minutes standing time and
   grilling time
SETTING: Full power (100%) and
   conventional grill

225 g/8 oz macaroni
1 tablespoon oil
1 teaspoon salt
1.75 litres/3 pints boiling water

SAUCE
2 garlic cloves, crushed
50 g/2 oz butter or margarine
50 g/2 oz plain flour
150 ml/$\frac{1}{4}$ pint tomato juice
450 ml/$\frac{3}{4}$ pint milk
1 level teaspoon dried chopped
   oregano
Salt and pepper to taste
3 tomatoes, sliced and 50 g/2 oz
   finely grated Cheddar cheese,
   to garnish

1 Place the macaroni, oil, salt and boiling water in a large bowl. Cook, covered, until the water comes back

to the boil, then cook for a further 9 minutes. Check during cooking that the macaroni is covered with the water. Stand, covered, for 8 minutes to finish off cooking.

2 For the sauce, place the garlic and butter or margarine in a large jug. Cook, uncovered, for 1 minute or until the butter or margarine has melted. Stir in the flour, then blend in the tomato juice, milk, oregano and salt and pepper to taste. Cook, uncovered, for 6 minutes or until thickened, stirring every minute.

3 Drain the macaroni well and stir it into the sauce.

4 Transfer to a warm fireproof serving dish, cover with a layer of tomato slices and sprinkle with the cheese. Brown under a conventional grill.

Freezing: Freeze after step 3. Use within 6 months.

Thawing: Full power (100%). Use a large bowl. Cook, covered, for 12 minutes or until the macaroni is completely heated through, gently breaking up and stirring it after 5 and 9 minutes. Continue from step 4.

TUNA WITH BUTTERFLY PASTA SALAD

For 4

This dish makes a filling cold main course to serve with a mixed green salad. Pasta shells can be used instead of butterfly pasta. The pasta can be frozen without the fish and vegetables, as the thawing process spoils their texture. This dish may be stored in the refrigerator overnight.

PREPARATION: About 10 minutes
COOKING: About 9 minutes, plus 10 minutes standing time
SETTING: Full power (100%)

106

1.75 litres/3 pints boiling water
1 tablespoon olive oil or vegetable oil
$\frac{1}{4}$ level teaspoon salt
1 garlic clove, crushed
275 g/10 oz butterfly pasta
198 g/7 oz can of tuna fish, drained and flaked with oil reserved
1 tablespoon white wine vinegar
6 spring onions, trimmed, washed and finely chopped
2 tomatoes, skinned and roughly chopped
4 canned anchovies, drained and roughly chopped
Freshly ground black pepper to taste
8 lettuce leaves, washed

1 Place the boiling water, oil, salt, garlic and pasta in a large bowl. Cook, covered, until the water comes back to the boil, then continue cooking for 9 minutes. Check during cooking that the pasta is still covered with the water. Set aside, covered, for 10 minutes to finish off the cooking process.

2 Drain in a colander and run cold water through the pasta. Drain again thoroughly and transfer to a bowl. Leave to cool.

3 Mix together the reserved oil from the can of tuna and the vinegar and toss into the cold pasta. Toss in the flaked fish, onions, tomatoes, anchovies and add pepper to taste.

4 Serve on a bed of lettuce.

Freezing: Freeze the pasta after step 1. Use within 6 months. (See page 50 for an easy-freeze method for pasta, using freezer bags.)

Thawing: Full power (100%). Place in a large bowl. Cook, covered, for 3 minutes to start the thawing process. Pour over 600 ml/1 pint boiling water. Cook, covered, for 3 minutes or until completely thawed but not heated. Separate the pasta and continue as from step 2.

TAGLIATELLE WITH CHEESE AND NUTS
For 4

This makes a filling main course. For a more economical dish, substitute finely grated Cheddar for the ricotta and Parmesan cheese. The pasta can be frozen without the cheese as cheese can go stringy during thawing.

PREPARATION: About 15 minutes
COOKING: About 9 minutes, plus 8
   minutes standing time
SETTING: Full power (100%)

225 g/8 oz tagliatelle
1 level teaspoon salt
1 tablespoon olive oil or
   vegetable oil
1.75 litres/3 pints boiling water
   75 ml/2½ fl oz double cream
225 g/8 oz ricotta cheese,
   crumbled
50 g/2 oz Parmesan cheese, finely
   grated
125 g/4 oz pecan nuts, finely
   chopped
Freshly ground black pepper to
   taste
50 g/2 oz butter or margarine,
   cut into small pieces

1 Place the tagliatelle, salt, oil and boiling water in a large bowl. Cook, covered, until the water comes back to the boil, then cook for a further 9 minutes. Check during cooking that the pasta is still covered with water. Set aside, covered, for 8 minutes to finish cooking.
2 Meanwhile, toss together the cream, ricotta cheese, Parmesan cheese, nuts and add pepper to taste.
3 Drain the tagliatelle and toss in the butter or margarine until melted. Toss in the cheese mixture and pile into a large warm serving dish.

Freezing: Freeze after step 1. Use within 6 months. (See page 50 for an easy-freeze method for pasta.)

Thawing: Full power (100%). Use a large bowl. Cook, covered, for 3 minutes to start the thawing process. Pour over 600 ml/1 pint boiling water and cook, covered, for 5 minutes or until completely heated through. Gently separate the tagliatelle halfway through cooking. Continue as from step 2.

VEGETABLE LASAGNE
For 4 to 6

This makes not only an excellent main course or supper dish, but it can be served for a hot buffet party. It is suitable for freezing but without the cheese topping, as cheese loses texture during thawing.

PREPARATION: About 15 minutes
COOKING: About 19 minutes, plus
   10 minutes standing time
SETTING: Full power (100%) and
   conventional grill

175 g/6 oz green lasagne
3 tablespoons olive oil or
   vegetable oil
1.2 litres/2 pints boiling
   vegetable or chicken stock, or
   water
2 garlic cloves, crushed
½ red pepper, seeds removed,
   finely diced
2 medium onions, peeled and
   finely chopped
1 level teaspoon dried mixed
   herbs
50 g/2 oz mushrooms, finely
   chopped
40 g/1½ oz plain flour
397 g/14 oz can of tomatoes,
   chopped, with juice
Salt and pepper to taste
50 g/2 oz Cheddar cheese, finely
   grated

1 Place the lasagne in a shallow fireproof dish measuring 33 by 19 by 5 cm/12 by 8 by 2 inches.

2 Add 1 tablespoon of the oil to 900 ml/1½ pints of the boiling stock. Pour this over the lasagne, making sure the pasta is completely covered. Cook, covered, until the stock comes back to the boil and cook for a further 9 minutes. Check from time to time that the pasta is still covered with water. Set aside, covered, for 10 minutes to finish cooking.

3 Place the garlic, red pepper, onions, herbs, mushrooms and remaining 2 tablespoons oil in a medium bowl. Cook, covered, for 5 minutes or until the onions are tender.

4 Stir in the flour. Gradually blend in the tomatoes and juice, the remaining stock, and salt and pepper to taste. Cook, uncovered, for 5 minutes or until thickened, stirring every minute to avoid lumps.

5 Drain the lasagne and arrange half over the base of the shallow fireproof dish. Pour over half the vegetable sauce. Cover with the remaining lasagne, then the rest of the sauce.

6 Sprinkle the cheese over and brown under a preheated grill.

Freezing: Freeze after step 5. Use within 6 months.

Thawing: Full power (100%) and Defrost (30%). Place in a shallow fireproof dish (33 by 19 by 5 cm/12 by 8 by 2 inches). Cook, covered, on Full power (100%) for 8 minutes, then stand for 10 minutes. Reduce to Defrost (30%) and cook, covered, for 20 minutes. Increase to Full power (100%) and continue cooking for 8 minutes, or until the lasagne is completely heated through. Continue as from step 6.

Note: This dish takes time to thaw because of the density of the pasta and sauce layers.

PURÉE OF BUTTER BEANS AND BACON
For 4

This can be used as an extra vegetable with roast or grilled meat. It can be frozen.

PREPARATION: About 5 minutes
COOKING: About 1 hour 16 minutes
SETTING: Full power (100%) and Defrost (30%)

225 g/8 oz dried butter beans
Cold water (see method)
4 rashers smoked streaky bacon, rinds removed, chopped
50 g/2 oz butter or margarine
Salt and pepper to taste
2 tablespoons double cream or milk
Sprigs of parsley to garnish

1 Place the butter beans in a bowl and cover with cold water. Leave to soak overnight. Drain.
2 Transfer the beans to a medium bowl, pour over 600 ml/1 pint water. Stir in the bacon. Cook, covered, for 4 minutes or until the water is boiling, then let it boil for a further 12 minutes.
3 Reduce power to Defrost (30%). Cook, covered, for 60 minutes or until the beans are tender.
4 Add the butter or margarine, salt and pepper to taste and the cream or milk. Put through a liquidiser or food processor until smooth, then spoon into a warm serving dish and garnish with sprigs of parsley.

Freezing: Freeze before garnishing. Use within 2 months.

Thawing: Full power (100%). Use a medium bowl. Cook, covered, for 10 minutes or until the purée is completely heated through, stirring halfway through cooking.

CURRIED RED LENTILS
For 4

This dish is suitable for freezing, and can be served with roast or grilled meat.

PREPARATION: About 5 minutes
COOKING: About 21 minutes, plus
   10 minutes standing time
SETTING: Full power (100%) and
   Defrost (30%)

225 g/8 oz red split lentils
½ level teaspoon salt
1 level teaspoon curry powder
Cold water (see method)
**50 g/2 butter or margarine, cut
   into pieces**

1 Place the lentils, salt and curry powder in a large bowl and add enough water to cover the lentils. Cook, covered, on Full power for 6 minutes or until boiling. Stir.
2 Reduce power to Defrost (30%). Cook, covered, for 15 minutes or until the lentils are tender, then let them stand, covered, for a further 10 minutes to finish cooking.
3 Drain if necessary, stir in the butter or margarine until it is melted.

Freezing: Use within 3 months.

Thawing: Full power (100%). Use a medium bowl. Cook, covered, for 10 minutes or until completely heated through, stirring halfway through cooking.

LENTIL PATTIES
For 4

A good way of serving extra fibre in the diet, these can be served with hamburgers, baked beans, or roast or grilled meat. They are suitable for freezing.

PREPARATION: About 10 minutes
COOKING: About 22 minutes, plus
   10 minutes standing time, plus
   frying time
SETTING: Full power (100%) and
   Defrost (30%) and conventional
   hob

**1 small onion, peeled and
   coarsely grated**
225 g/8 oz red split lentils
Cold water (see method)
1 egg (size 2), lightly beaten
**50 g/2 oz fresh white
   breadcrumbs**
Salt and pepper to taste

COATING
6 tablespoons milk
50 g/2 oz dried breadcrumbs
Oil for frying

1 Cook the onion in a large bowl, covered, on full power for 1½ minutes to soften the onion.
2 Stir in the lentils and add sufficient cold water to cover. Cook, covered, for 6 minutes or until boiling. Stir.
3 Reduce power to Defrost (30%). Cook, covered, for 15 minutes or until the lentils are tender. Stand, covered, for 10 minutes to finish off cooking.
4 Drain. Put the lentils through a liquidiser or food processor with the egg and work until smooth. Stir in the breadcrumbs and salt and pepper to taste.
5 Use a lightly floured board and shape the mixture into 8 patties measuring approximately 5 cm/2 inches in diameter and 2.5 cm/1 inch thick. Brush each with milk and coat in dried breadcrumbs.
6 Heat the oil in a frying pan, on the conventional hob. Fry until golden brown on both sides.
Freezing: Use within 3 months.
Thawing: Full power (100%). Arrange in a circle on a piece of kitchen paper towel on a plate. Cook, uncovered, for 7½ minutes or until the patties are completely heated through. Rearrange and turn them over after 5 minutes.

110

Chapter 9
Vegetables

JERUSALEM ARTICHOKES WITH CHEESE SAUCE

For 4

Use a Herb sauce (page 118) instead of the Cheese sauce. It can't be frozen as the sauce turns thin and watery during thawing.

PREPARATION: About 10 minutes
COOKING: About 14 minutes
SETTING: Full power (100%)

450 g/1 lb Jerusalem artichokes, scrubbed or peeled and thinly sliced
3 tablespoons water
A pinch of salt

SAUCE
25 g/1 oz butter or margarine
25 g/1 oz plain flour
300 ml/½ pint milk
Salt and pepper to taste
1 level teaspoon prepared English mustard
50 g/2 oz Cheddar cheese, finely grated
Chopped fresh parsley, to garnish

1 Put the artichokes in a large bowl. Toss them in the water and salt. Cook, covered, for 9 minutes or until tender, stirring halfway through cooking. Set aside, covered, while making the sauce.
2 Put the butter or margarine into a small jug. Cook, uncovered, for 1 minute or until melted. Blend in the flour, then slowly stir in the milk, salt and pepper to taste and mustard. Cook, uncovered, for 3 minutes or until thickened, stirring every minute.
3 Stir in the cheese. Cook for a further 1 minute, if necessary, to melt the cheese.
4 Drain the artichokes, arrange them in warm serving dish and pour over the sauce. Garnish with chopped parsley.
Freezing: Not suitable.

STIR-FRIED VEGETABLES

Serves 4 as an accompaniment, or makes a substantial dish for 2 or 3 if tossed with hot cooked noodles

Stir-fried vegetables should be quite crisp but the recipe lets the cook decide the degree of cooking required. This dish is better freshly made to ensure that the vegetables stay crisp.

PREPARATION: About 15 minutes
COOKING: About 6 minutes
SETTING: Full power (100%)

1 garlic clove, crushed
1 bunch spring onions, trimmed and left whole, or 1 leek, washed, trimmed and sliced
125 g/4 oz carrots, peeled and cut into large matchsticks
1 stick celery, trimmed and cut into large matchsticks
1 red or green pepper, seeds removed, cut into large matchsticks
2 tablespoons olive oil or vegetable oil
1 tablespoon soy sauce
125 g/4 oz button mushrooms, finely sliced
Salt and pepper to taste

1 Combine the garlic, onions or leek, carrots, celery, red or green pepper, oil and soy sauce in a large bowl. Cook, covered, for 4 minutes or until the vegetables are slightly softened, stirring halfway through cooking.
2 Stir in the mushrooms, and salt and pepper to taste. Cook, covered, for 2 minutes or until the vegetables are the desired texture.
Freezing: Not suitable.

BROCCOLI WITH LEMON BUTTER
For 4

Vary the recipe by omitting the butter or margarine, the lemon juice and rind and serving the broccoli with Hollandaise sauce (page 118). It can't be frozen, as the broccoli goes limp.

PREPARATION: About 10 minutes
COOKING: About 10 minutes, plus 5 minutes standing time
SETTING: Full power (100%)

3 tablespoons water
A pinch of salt
450 g/1 lb fresh broccoli, stalks split lengthways
125 g/4 oz butter or margarine, cut into knobs
Juice and finely grated rind of $\frac{1}{2}$ a lemon
Salt and pepper to taste

1 Put the water into a large bowl and add salt. Place the broccoli in the bowl with the flower heads downwards and the stalks upright. Cook, covered, for 7 minutes, then set aside, covered, for 5 minutes.
2 Check if the stalks are tender. If necessary, return to the cooker for 1 to 2 minutes or until the stalks are tender.
3 Place the butter or margarine, lemon juice and rind, and salt and pepper to taste in a small bowl. Cook, uncovered, for 3 minutes or until the butter or margarine has melted.

4 Drain the broccoli, arrange in a warm serving dish and pour the melted butter over.
Freezing: Not suitable.

COURGETTES WITH TOMATOES AND FRESH ROSEMARY
For 4

Suitable for freezing. For a change of flavour, use chopped parsley or dill instead.

PREPARATION: About 15 minutes
COOKING: About 11 minutes
SETTING: Full power (100%)

1 medium onion, peeled and thinly sliced
1 garlic clove, crushed
25 g/1 oz butter or margarine, cut into pieces
325 g/12 oz courgettes, trimmed and thinly sliced
225 g/8 oz tomatoes, skinned and roughly chopped
1 rounded tablespoon tomato purée
1 level teaspoon freshly chopped rosemary
Salt and pepper to taste

1 Place the onion, garlic and butter or margarine in a large bowl. Cook, covered, for 3 minutes or until onions are softened.
2 Into the onion mixture, stir the courgettes, tomatoes, tomato purée, rosemary and salt and pepper to taste. Cook, covered, for 8 minutes or until the courgettes are tender, stirring halfway through cooking.
Freezing: Use within 6 months.
Thawing: Full power (100%). Use a large bowl. Cook, covered, for 8 minutes or until the vegetables are completely heated through, stirring after 5 and 6 minutes.

CARROTS IN ORANGE

For 4

This is suitable for freezing.

PREPARATION: About 10 minutes
COOKING: About $7\frac{1}{2}$ minutes
SETTING: Full power (100%)

Finely grated rind of $\frac{1}{2}$ an orange
3 tablespoons fresh or
   unsweetened orange juice
$\frac{1}{2}$ level teaspoon caster sugar
450 g/1 lb carrots, peeled or
   scrubbed and thinly sliced
25 g/1 oz butter or margarine,
   cut into pieces

1 Put the orange rind, juice, sugar
and carrots in a medium bowl. Cook,
covered, for $7\frac{1}{2}$ minutes or until the
carrots are tender, stirring halfway
through cooking.
2 Drain, then toss in the butter or
margarine until melted. Spoon into a
warm serving dish.

Freezing: Use within 6 months.

Thawing: Full power (100%). Use a
medium bowl. Cook, covered, for 9
minutes or until the carrots are
completely heated through, stirring
after 4 and 6 minutes.

FENNEL IN BUTTER

For 4

*You can leave out the butter and serve
this with a Cheese sauce (page 112). It
is suitable for freezing, unless you use
Cheese sauce – which will thin and turn
watery during thawing.*

PREPARATION: About 5 minutes
COOKING: About 8 minutes, plus 4
   minutes standing time
SETTING: Full power (100%)

450 g/1 lb fennel, trimmed and
   thinly sliced
4 tablespoons water
A pinch of salt
25 g/1 oz butter or margarine,
   cut into pieces

1 Put the fennel in a medium bowl.
Toss it in salted water, then cook,
covered, for 8 minutes or until tender,
stirring halfway through cooking.
2 Let it stand, covered, for 4 minutes
to finish cooking. Then drain, toss in
butter or margarine until melted and
spoon into a warm serving dish.
Freezing: Use within 6 months.
Thawing: Full power (100%). Use a
medium bowl. Cook, covered, for 10
minutes or until the fennel is
completely heated through, stirring
halfway through cooking.

LEEKS WITH BUTTER

For 4

*For a change, leave out the butter and
serve with a Herb sauce (page 118) or
Cheese sauce (page 112). Suitable for
freezing, unless Cheese sauce is used (see
previous recipe).*

PREPARATION: About 10 minutes
COOKING: About 10 minutes, plus 5
   minutes standing time
SETTING: Full power (100%)

575 g/1$\frac{1}{4}$ lb leeks, trimmed and
   finely sliced into rings
3 tablespoons water
A pinch of salt
40 g/1$\frac{1}{2}$ oz butter or margarine,
   cut into pieces
1 level tablespoon freshly
   chopped parsley, to garnish

1 Place the leeks in a large bowl.
Toss them in the water with a pinch
of salt. Cook, covered, for 10 minutes
or until tender, stirring halfway
through cooking. Set aside, covered,
for 5 minutes to finish cooking.

2 Drain the leeks and toss in the butter or margarine until this has melted. Arrange the leeks in a warm dish and garnish with chopped parsley.

Freezing: Freeze before garnishing. Use within 6 months.

Thawing: Full power (100%). Use a large bowl. Cook, covered, for 9 minutes or until the leeks are completely heated through, stirring halfway through cooking.

MANGE TOUT OR SUGAR PEAS
For 4

If following a low-fat diet, leave out the butter or margarine. These peas are suitable for freezing.

PREPARATION: About 5 minutes
COOKING: About 8 minutes, plus 5 minutes standing time
SETTING: Full power (100%)

325 g/12 oz mange tout, trimmed and any strings removed
3 tablespoons water
A pinch of salt
15 g/$\frac{1}{2}$ oz butter or margarine, cut into pieces

1 Place the mange tout in a large bowl. Toss in the water and a pinch of salt. Cook, covered, for 8 minutes or until tender, stirring halfway through cooking.
2 Let the peas stand, covered, for 5 minutes. Then drain, toss in the butter or margarine until it has melted. Spoon the peas into a warm serving dish.

Freezing: Use within 6 months.

Thawing: Full power (100%). Use a medium bowl. Cook, covered, for 12 minutes or until the mange tout are completely heated through, stirring halfway through cooking.

PEAS WITH HAM AND LETTUCE
For 4

For a change, use cooked crumbled crispy bacon instead of ham. This dish is suitable for freezing.

PREPARATION: About 10 minutes
COOKING: About 14 minutes
SETTING: Full power (100%)

25 g/1 oz butter or margarine
1 medium onion, finely chopped
25 g/1 oz cooked ham, cut into fine strips
1 lettuce leaf, finely shredded
450 g/1 lb frozen peas
Salt to taste

1 Place the butter or margarine and onion in a medium bowl. Cook, covered, for 3 minutes or until tender, stirring and checking after 2 minutes.
2 Stir in the ham, lettuce and frozen peas, then cook, covered, for 9 minutes or until the peas are tender, stirring halfway through cooking.
3 Add salt to taste and transfer peas into a warm serving dish.

Freezing: Use within 6 months.

Thawing: Full power (100%). Use a medium bowl. Cook, covered, for 9 minutes or until all is completely heated through, stirring halfway through cooking.

GARLIC JACKET POTATOES
For 4

Suitable for freezing. Try other fillings, such as two tablespoons of cooked, crumbled crispy bacon or chopped ham, or finely grated cheese for each potato.

PREPARATION: About 5 minutes
COOKING: About 16 minutes, plus 5 minutes standing time
SETTING: Full power (100%)

4 medium potatoes, total weight 1 kg/2½ lb, scrubbed, dried and pricked with a fork
25 g/1 oz butter or margarine
At least 3 garlic cloves, crushed
Salt and pepper to taste
2 tablespoons double cream or milk
Sprigs of parsley, to garnish

1 Arrange the potatoes in a circle on a piece of kitchen paper in the cooker.
2 Cook, uncovered, for 13 minutes or until soft to the touch, turning over halfway through cooking. Remove the potatoes and wrap each one tightly in foil. Leave to stand for 5 minutes.
3 Remove the potatoes from the foil. Slice the top off each potato and scoop out the flesh. Mash the flesh with the butter or margarine, garlic, salt and pepper and cream or milk. Pile the potato back into the skins.
4 Cook, uncovered, for 3 minutes to reheat. Garnish with sprigs of parsley for serving.
Freezing: Freeze before garnishing. Use within 2 months.
Thawing: Full power (100%). Arrange the potatoes in a circle on a piece of kitchen towel on a plate. Cook, uncovered, for 17 minutes or until the potatoes are completely reheated through. Rearrange the potatoes after 8 minutes.

CREAMED PARSNIPS
Makes 4 to 6 helpings

This method of cooking makes a pleasant change to serving roast parsnips. It is suitable for freezing.

PREPARATION: About 10 minutes
COOKING: About 11 minutes
SETTING: Full power (100%)

675 g/1½ lb parsnips, peeled or scrubbed and thinly sliced
3 tablespoons water
15 g/½ oz butter or margarine
1½ tablespoons single cream or milk
Salt and pepper to taste
Sprigs of parsley, to garnish

1 Put the parsnips in a large bowl with the water. Cook, covered, for 9 minutes or until tender, stirring halfway through cooking.
2 Put the parsnips, water, butter or margarine, cream or milk, and salt and pepper through a liquidiser or food processor until smooth.
3 Transfer to a warm serving dish and reheat for 2 minutes, if necessary. Garnish with sprigs of parsley.
Freezing: Freeze before garnishing. Use within 6 months.
Thawing: Full power (100%). Use a large bowl and cook, covered, for 8 minutes or until the parsnips are completely heated through. Stir after 2 and 4 minutes.

Chapter 10
Sauces
Savoury and
Sweet

BARBECUE SAUCE
Makes about 300 ml/½ pint

This spicy sauce is delicious with hamburgers, spare ribs or poached white fish. It is suitable for freezing.

PREPARATION: About 5 minutes
COOKING: About 6 minutes
SETTING: Full power (100%)

1 tablespoon sesame oil
1 medium onion, peeled and finely chopped
2 garlic cloves, crushed
1 level tablespoon cornflour
150 ml/¼ pint tomato juice
150 ml/¼ pint hot chicken stock
2 tablespoons red wine vinegar
1 teaspoon Tabasco sauce
1 teaspoon Worcestershire sauce
75 g/3 oz soft dark brown sugar

1 Place the oil, onion and garlic in a large jug. Cook, covered, for 3 minutes or until the onion is soft.
2 Blend together the cornflour and tomato juice and stir in the hot stock, vinegar, Tabasco sauce, Worcestershire sauce and sugar.
3 Stir the cornflour mixture into the onion mixture. Cook, uncovered, for 3 minutes or until thickened, stirring every minute.
Freezing: Use within 6 months.
Thawing: Full power (100%). Use a small jug. Cook, uncovered, for 5 minutes or until boiling, stirring every 2 minutes. Beat well before serving.

HERB SAUCE
Makes about 300 ml/½ pint

This sauce is suitable to serve over vegetables or as an accompaniment to poached white fish or grilled steak. It is suitable for freezing.

PREPARATION: About 10 minutes

COOKING: About 5 minutes
SETTING: Full power (100%)

25 g/1 oz butter or margarine
25 g/1 oz plain flour
300 ml/½ pint milk
1 egg yolk
Salt and pepper to taste
1 level teaspoon chopped fresh tarragon
1 level teaspoon chopped capers
1 level teaspoon chopped fresh dill
1 level teaspoon chopped fresh parsley

1 Place the butter or margarine in a small jug. Cook, uncovered, for a minute or until melted. Stir in the flour. Gradually blend in the milk and cook, uncovered, for 4 minutes or until thickened, stirring every minute.
2 Beat in the egg yolk, salt and pepper to taste. Stir in the tarragon, capers, dill and parsley.
Freezing: Use within 1 month.
Thawing: Full power (100%). Use a small jug and cook, uncovered, for 5 minutes or until boiling. Break up and stir after 2 and 4 minutes. Beat well before serving.

HOLLANDAISE SAUCE
Makes about 150 ml/¼ pint

This classic sauce is perfect with poached, steamed or grilled white fish and salmon, poached eggs, broccoli or asparagus. It is not suitable for freezing or storing in the refrigerator as it separates and loses texture.

PREPARATION: About 5 minutes
COOKING: About 2 minutes
SETTING: Full power (100%)

125 g/4 oz unsalted butter, cut into pieces
1 tablespoon lemon juice

2 (size 3) egg yolks, at room
 temperature
½ teaspoon dry English mustard
A pinch of cayenne pepper

1 Put the butter in a small bowl.
Cook, uncovered, for 1½ minutes or
until just melted.
2 Whisk in the lemon juice, yolks,
mustard and cayenne pepper. Cook,
uncovered, for 30 seconds. Beat well.
Be careful not to overcook as the
sauce will curdle.
3 The sauce should coat the back of
a spoon. If necessary return to the
microwave for 10 second bursts,
beating hard in between. Serve
immediately.
Freezing: Not suitable.

SWEET
MOUSSELINE
SAUCE
For 2 to 4

*A superb sauce to serve with mousses
and soufflés. It is not suitable for
freezing or storing in the refrigerator as
it loses its light fluffy texture.*

PREPARATION: About 5 minutes
COOKING: About 30 seconds
SETTING: Full power (100%)

2 (size 1) egg yolks, at room
 temperature
4 tablespoons double cream
1 tablespoon dry white wine
1 to 2 teaspoons caster sugar
2 (size 1) egg whites, stiffly
 whisked

1 Place the yolks in a small bowl, and
lightly beat. Cook, uncovered, for 30
seconds, then whisk until thick and
creamy.
2 Gently fold in the cream, wine and
salt and pepper to taste. Fold in the
egg whites and serve at once.

Freezing: Not suitable.

Note: For a savoury version of this
sauce, substitute salt and pepper to
taste for the sugar. Serve with fish
and vegetable dishes.

HOT BRANDY SAUCE

Makes about 450 ml/¾ pint

Serve with fruit puddings, Christmas puddings and mince pies. It is suitable for freezing but when thawed, the sauce will need extra milk as it thickens on freezing.

PREPARATION: About 5 minutes
COOKING: About 4½ minutes
SETTING: Full power (100%)

3 level tablespoons cornflour
450 ml/¾ pint milk
2 tablespoons caster sugar
1 tablespoon single cream
3 tablespoons brandy

1 Blend the cornflour with 3 tablespoons of the milk.
2 Put the remaining milk and sugar into a large jug and cook for 2½ minutes or until the milk is hot. Stir the hot milk into the cornflour mixture.
3 Pour the milk back into the large jug and cook for 2 minutes or until thickened, stirring halfway through cooking.
4 Stir in the cream and brandy.
Freezing: Use within 1 month.
Thawing: Full power (100%). Use a large jug. Cook, uncovered, for 6 minutes, breaking up with a fork after 3 minutes. Beat in 5 tablespoons of milk after a further 2 minutes, then continue the cooking process. Whisk well before serving.

CHERRY SAUCE

Makes about 300 ml/½ pint

Serve hot with pancakes, or plain sweet steamed puddings, or cold with ice cream. It is suitable for freezing or storing in the refrigerator.

PREPARATION: About 5 minutes
COOKING: About 3 minutes
SETTING: Full power (100%)

Juice of ½ a lemon
2 tablespoons sweet sherry
About 220 ml/7½ fl oz water
2 level teaspoons arrowroot
25 g/1 oz caster sugar
1 rounded teaspoon redcurrant jelly
A few drops of red food colouring
40 g/1½ oz glacé cherries, roughly chopped

1 Mix together the lemon juice and sherry, then make up with water to 250 ml/8 fl oz.
2 Put the arrowroot in a small jug. Blend in a little of the liquid to make a smooth paste. Add the remaining liquid, sugar, redcurrant jelly and a little red colouring, taking care not to over-colour it.
3 Cook, uncovered, for 2 minutes or until boiling, stirring halfway through cooking.
4 Stir in the cherries and continue to cook for 1 minute or until the cherries are warmed through.
Freezing: Use within 6 months.
Thawing: Full power (100%). Use a large jug and cook, uncovered, for 5 minutes or until boiling. Break up after 2 minutes.

CHOCOLATE SAUCE

Makes about 300 ml/½ pint

A superb sauce to serve with sponge puddings, steamed chocolate puddings, pancakes or ice cream. It is suitable for freezing or it may be stored in the refrigerator and served cold.

PREPARATION: About 5 minutes
COOKING: About 4 minutes
SETTING: Full power (100%)

175 g/6 oz golden granulated or demerara sugar
75 g/3 oz cocoa powder
2 heaped teaspoons cornflour
A few drops of vanilla essence

285 ml/½ pint can of evaporated
milk
25 g/1 oz butter, chopped

1 Put the sugar, cocoa and cornflour
into a large jug. Slowly stir in the
vanilla essence and milk. Cook,
uncovered, for 4 minutes or until
thickened, stirring every minute.
3 Beat in the butter until it has
melted, and serve.
Freezing: Use within 6 months.
Thawing: Full power (100%). Use a
small jug. Cook, uncovered, for 4½
minutes or until boiling, stirring every
minute. Beat well before serving.

SWEET RED WINE SAUCE
Makes about 150 ml/¼ pint

*A delightful sauce to serve with
pancakes, poached fruit or steamed
sweet puddings. For a change, make a
sherry sauce by substituting apricot jam
for the raspberry jam and a medium or
sweet sherry for the red wine – in which
case omit the red colouring. The sauce
is suitable for freezing.*

PREPARATION: About 5 minutes
COOKING: About 4 minutes
SETTING: Full power (100%)

150 ml/¼ pint water
25 g/1 oz caster sugar
Juice and rind of ¼ of a lemon
2 tablespoons raspberry jam
1 level teaspoon arrowroot
2 tablespoons claret or
    medium-dry red wine
A few drops of red food
    colouring

1 Reserve 2 tablespoons of the water
to mix with the arrowroot later on.
Place the remaining water, sugar,
lemon juice, rind and jam in a small
jug. Cook, uncovered, for 3 minutes,
or until the sugar has dissolved,
stirring halfway through cooking.

2 Mix together the arrowroot and
reserved water to make a paste.
Gradually add the heated liquid to the
arrowroot mixture, stirring all the
time. Pour the sauce back into the
small jug and cook, uncovered, for 1
minute until clear, stirring halfway
through cooking.
3 Add the claret or wine and one or
two drops of red colouring, taking
care not to over-colour the sauce.
Strain and reheat if necessary.
Freezing: Use within 6 months.
Thawing: Full power (100%). Use a
small jug. Cook, uncovered, for 4
minutes or until boiling. Break up
with a fork after 1½ minutes.

BUTTERSCOTCH SAUCE
Makes about 150 ml/¼ pint

*A delicious sauce to serve with
pancakes, sweet steamed puddings or ice
cream. It is suitable for freezing and
it can be stored in the refrigerator, but
it will solidify. Once reheated, however,
it will turn runny.*

PREPARATION: About 5 minutes
COOKING: About 3 minutes
SETTING: Full power (100%)

75 g/3 oz butter, cut into pieces
50 g/2 oz soft light brown sugar
2 tablespoons golden syrup
1 teaspoon lemon juice

1 Place the butter, sugar and syrup
in a large jug. Cook, uncovered, for 2
minutes or until the sugar has almost
dissolved.
2 Stir well until all the sugar has
dissolved. Cook, uncovered, for 1
minute or until bubbling.
3 Stir in the lemon juice and pour
into a warm jug.
Freezing: Use within 6 months.
Thawing: Full power (100%). Use a
small jug. Cook, uncovered, for 1½
minutes or until boiling, stirring after
1 minute.

ORANGE CHUTNEY
Makes about 1.5 kg/3 lb

This is an unusual chutney to serve with cold meats or poultry. The orange flavour also makes it a perfect partner for a hard cheese.

PREPARATION TIME: About 15 minutes
COOKING: About 65 minutes
SETTING: Full power (100%)

675 g/1½ lb thin-skinned oranges, rind removed with a zester and retained
325 g/12 oz onions, peeled and chopped
325 g/12 oz cooking apples, peeled and chopped
225 g/8 oz sultanas
1 garlic clove, crushed
450 ml/¾ pint white wine vinegar
½ level teaspoon ground ginger
½ level teaspoon salt
1 level teaspoon ground mixed spice
¼ level teaspoon grated nutmeg
200 g/7 oz soft dark brown sugar
25 g/1 oz clear honey

1 Peel oranges, remove pips and discard. Roughly chop the fruit into small pieces.
2 Put the orange rind, oranges, onions and apples in a large bowl. Cook, covered, for 10 minutes or until onions have softened.
3 Stir in the sultanas, garlic, vinegar, ginger, salt, spice, nutmeg, sugar and honey. Cook, uncovered, for 55 minutes or until thick, stirring several times during cooking. The correct consistency is reached when a wooden spoon is drawn across the base of the bowl and the line can be defined.

4 Pour the hot chutney into three 450 g/1 lb warm sterilised jars. Cover with plastic lids or jam pot covers. Ensure the lids are air-tight. Leave to cool. Label.
Freezing: Not suitable.

APRICOT JAM
Makes about 1.5 kg/3 lb

A delicious jam to serve with scones and bread. Do not exceed the given quantities as there would be a risk of the bubbling mixture boiling over during cooking.

PREPARATION: About 15 minutes
COOKING: About 30 minutes
SETTING: Full power (100%)

675 g/1½ lb fresh apricots, cut in half and stones removed
8 stones, with shells removed and kernels blanched
65 ml/2½ fl oz cold strained tea
675 g/1½ lb preserving sugar

1 Put the apricots, kernels and tea into a large bowl. Cook, covered, for 10 minutes or until the fruit is cooked.
2 Stir in the sugar until dissolved. Cook, uncovered, for 20 minutes or until setting point is reached.
3 To test for setting. Place ½ tablespoon of jam on to a cold saucer and allow to cool. Push the edge of the jam with a fingertip. If the jam wrinkles or 'frills', setting point is reached. Stand, uncovered, for 10 minutes.
4 Spoon into three 450 g/1 lb warm sterilised jars. Cool. Place a wax paper disc over the jam, cover the lid. Label.
Freezing: Not suitable.

Chapter 11
Puddings

JAM SPONGE PUDDINGS
For 4

These puddings must be served as soon as they are cooked. If allowed to cool, they will lose moisture and harden. For this reason, they are not suitable for freezing.

PREPARATION: About 10 minutes
COOKING: About 4 minutes
SETTING: Full power (100%)

50 g/2 oz butter or margarine
50 g/2 oz caster sugar
1 (size 2) egg, lightly beaten
75 g/3 oz self-raising flour
1 tablespoon milk
2 drops vanilla essence
3 level tablespoons jam

1 Cream the butter or margarine and sugar together until light and fluffy. Beat in the egg. Fold in the flour, milk and vanilla essence.
2 Spread the jam inside four greased 150-ml/¼-pint ramekin dishes or four large cups or mugs. Cook, uncovered, for 1 minute or until the jam is liquid and hot.
3 Spoon the sponge mixture over the jam. Cover loosely with clear film and arrange the dishes in a circle in the cooker. Cook for about 3 minutes or until a dry knife inserted comes out clean. Remove any which are cooked before 3 minutes. Rearrange the dishes halfway through cooking.
4 Loosen the puddings with a knife and turn out on to a warm serving dish. Serve immediately.
Freezing: Not suitable.

PLUM CRUMBLE
For 4

The breadcrumbs and butter make this crumble deliciously different. Apples can be used instead of plums. The pudding is suitable for freezing but the topping will not be so crisp.

PREPARATION: About 15 minutes
COOKING: About 10 minutes, plus frying time
SETTING: Full power (100%) and conventional hob

800 g/1¾ lb plums (unstoned weight), stones removed
75 g/3 oz caster sugar

TOPPING
125 g/4 oz plain flour
50 g/2 oz dark brown sugar
50 g/2 oz margarine
50 g/2 oz butter
50 g/2 oz fresh white breadcrumbs

1 Arrange the plums and sugar in a 1.6-litre/2¾-pint round soufflé dish.
2 For the topping, rub together the plain flour, sugar and margarine until the mixture resembles fine breadcrumbs.
3 Sprinkle over the fruit and make several holes in the mixture to allow for the escape of steam. Cook, uncovered, for 10 minutes or until the fruit is cooked, turning the container halfway through to ensure even cooking. Set aside and keep warm if serving hot.
4 Melt the butter in a frying pan on a conventional hob. Stir in the breadcrumbs and fry until golden brown, stirring all the time to avoid overbrowning.
5 Sprinkle the fried crumbs over the crumble. Serve hot or cold.

Freezing: Freeze after step 3. Use within 6 months.

Thawing: Full power (100%) and Defrost (30%). Place in a 1.6-litre/2¾-pint round soufflé dish. Cook, uncovered, on Defrost (30%) for 15 minutes, then let it stand for 20 minutes. Continue to cook on Full power (100%) for 15 minutes or until heated completely through. Continue from step 4.

CHOCOLATE BRANDY FUDGE CAKE

Makes 8 slices

This rich cake is best eaten on the day it is cooked, but it can be frozen without the fudge topping (the topping loses texture during thawing).

PREPARATION: About 10 minutes
COOKING: About 10½ minutes, plus 5 minutes standing time and 30 minutes refrigeration
SETTING: Full power (100%)

CAKE
175 g/6 oz soft margarine
175 g/6 oz dark brown (Muscovado) sugar
40 g/1½ oz cocoa powder
150 g/5 oz self-raising flour
1 level teaspoon baking powder
1 tablespoon brandy
2 tablespoons milk
3 (size 1) eggs, lightly beaten

TOPPING
25 g/1 oz cocoa powder
2 tablespoons brandy
About 6 tablespoons water
2 teaspoons milk
50 g/2 oz dark brown (Muscovado) sugar
25 g/1 oz butter
225 g/8 oz icing sugar, sieved

1 For the cake: Mix together the margarine, Muscovado sugar, cocoa powder, flour, baking powder, 1 tablespoon brandy, milk and eggs until smooth. Be very careful not to overbeat the mixture or the cake will not rise.
2 Butter an 18-cm/7-inch round container that is 9 cm/3½ inches deep. Line the base with buttered, greaseproof paper, then spoon in the mixture. Stand the cake on an upturned microproof plate and cook,
uncovered, for 6 minutes or until the mixture is cooked (it should be soft and springy to the touch). Turn the container round halfway through cooking to ensure that the mixture rises evenly.
3 Let the cake stand for 5 minutes before loosening the edges and turning it out on to a cooling rack covered with greaseproof paper. Remove the greaseproof lining paper from the cake and leave the cake upside down to cool completely.
4 Put the cake in a refrigerator or freezer for 30 minutes to make it easier to ice – the crumbs on the outside of the cake will be firm.
5 Now for the topping: In a medium bowl, mix the cocoa powder with 1 tablespoon brandy and 2 tablespoons cold water until smooth. Add the milk, sugar and butter and cook, uncovered, for 4½ minutes or until the mixture is bubbling, stirring halfway through cooking.
6 Beat in half the icing sugar with 1 tablespoon brandy. Beat in the remaining sugar and add sufficient water to obtain a slack but not runny mixture. Beat well for 4 minutes.
7 Spoon the warm icing over the cake and use a warm wet knife to spread it quickly over the top and sides.
Freezing: Freeze after step 4. Use within 6 months.
Thawing: Full power (100%). Stand on a piece of kitchen paper on a plate. Cook, uncovered, for 1 minute to start the thawing process. Stand for 20 to 30 minutes at room temperature or until thawed. Continue from step 5.

COFFEE GATEAU
Makes 8 slices

This gâteau is best eaten on the day it is cooked but it can be frozen, if necessary.

PREPARATION: About 15 minutes
COOKING: About 6 minutes, plus 5 minutes standing time and 30 minutes refrigeration

SETTING: Full power (100%)

CAKE
175 g/6 oz soft margarine
175 g/6 oz caster sugar
175 g/6 oz self-raising flour
1 level teaspoon baking powder
3 (size 1) eggs
1 tablespoon milk
2 tablespoons coffee essence

TOPPING
175 g/6 oz butter
325 g/12 oz icing sugar, sieved
2 tablespoons coffee essence
75 g/3 oz walnuts, finely
** chopped**

1 Put the margarine, sugar, flour, baking powder, eggs, milk and 2 tablespoons coffee essence into a bowl. Beat well until the mixture is smooth, but be careful not to overbeat or the cake will not rise.

2 Butter or oil an 18-cm/7-inch round, 9-cm/3½-inch deep container. Line the bottom with buttered or oiled greaseproof paper. Spoon in the mixture. Stand the container on an upturned plate or pie dish and cook, uncovered, for 6 minutes or until the mixture is cooked. Turn the container round halfway through cooking to ensure that the mixture will rise evenly. When cooked, the top should be soft and springy to the touch and a knife inserted through the cake should come out clean.

3 Let it stand for 5 minutes before loosening the edges and turning the cake out on to a cooling rack covered with greaseproof paper. Remove the lining paper and leave the cake upside down to cool completely.

4 Put the cake in the refrigerator or freezer for 30 minutes as this will make icing easier – the crumbs on the outside of the cake will be firm.

5 Meanwhile, make the topping. Cream together the butter, icing sugar and coffee essence until smooth.

6 Reserve a little of the icing for the decoration, and spread the rest of the icing over the top and sides of the cake. Roll the sides of the cake in the chopped walnuts.

7 Using a large potato star icing nozzle, decorate the top of the cake.
Freezing: Use within 6 months.
Thawing: Full power (100%). Stand on a piece of kitchen paper on a plate. Cook, uncovered, for 1 minute to start the thawing process. Stand for 20 to 30 minutes at room temperature or until thawed.

CHILLED MOCHA PUDDING
For 4 to 6

This becomes a special occasion pudding with 2 tablespoons of brandy added to the warmed coffee, and served with Sweet mousseline sauce (page 119). It is suitable for freezing. If frozen with the cream, reduce the storage time to 2 months.

PREPARATION: About 10 minutes, plus 2–3 hours refrigeration
COOKING: About 4½ to 5 minutes, plus 10 minutes standing time
SETTING: Full power (100%)

125 g/4 oz soft margarine
125 g/4 oz caster sugar
25 g/1 oz cocoa powder
90 g/3½ oz self-raising flour
1 level teaspoon baking powder
2 (size 1) eggs
150 ml/¼ pint warm coffee
Sugar to taste
150 ml/¼ pint double cream, to
** decorate**

1 Beat together the margarine, caster sugar, cocoa powder, flour, baking powder and eggs, until smooth. Avoid overbeating. Spoon into a 900-ml/1½-pint basin lined with clear film.
2 Stand the basin on an upturned

microproof plate, pie dish or rack.
Cook, covered, for 4½ to 5 minutes or
until the base of the pudding is
cooked. Check this by inserting a dry
sharp knife right down to the base –
it should come out clean. Set aside,
covered with a plate, for 10 minutes.
3 Mix together the warm coffee and
sugar to taste. Prick the pudding and
pour the coffee over. Refrigerate for
2 to 3 hours, or until chilled.
4 Turn the pudding on to a chilled
serving plate and decorate with
whipped cream.
Freezing: Freeze after step 3. Use
within 6 months. The pudding can
be frozen after decoration; use within
2 months.
Thawing: Full power (100%). Stand
on a plate. Cook, uncovered, for 1
minute. Stand for 30 minutes.
Continue from step 4. If frozen after
decoration, thaw at room
temperature.

LEMON CHEESECAKE
Makes 8 to 10 slices

*This delicious cheesecake can be served
all year round. It is important to use the
egg sizes given as they make the main
contribution to the 'set' of the mixture.*

PREPARATION: About 15 minutes
COOKING: About 7 minutes, plus
   refrigeration 3 to 4 hours
SETTING: Full power (100%)

BASE
75 g/3 oz butter or margarine
175 g/6 oz digestive biscuits,
   crushed

FILLING
450 g/1 lb full fat cream cheese
50 g/2 oz caster sugar
1 level tablespoon good quality
   bought, or homemade, lemon
   curd
Rind of 2 lemons, finely grated
2 (size 1) eggs, lightly beaten

DECORATION
Crystallised lemon slices

1 Put the butter in a small jug. Cook,
uncovered, for 1 minute or until
melted. Stir in the biscuits. Sprinkle
the crumbs over the base of a 23-cm/
9-inch flan dish. Press well down over
the base with the back of a metal
spoon.
2 Put the cheese, sugar, curd and
lemon rind in a medium bowl. Beat
in the eggs one at a time.
3 Cook, uncovered, for 6 minutes,
beating well after 2 and 4 minutes.
After cooking, beat the mixture until
smooth. Spoon over the biscuit
mixture and smooth over. Refrigerate
for 3 to 4 hours or until well chilled.
4 Decorate with slices of crystallised
lemon.

Freezing: Freeze after step 3 in the
flan dish. Use within 6 months.

Thawing: Defrost (30%). Cook,
uncovered, for 4 minutes. Stand for
30 minutes or until thawed. Continue
at step 4.

LEMON SOUFFLES
For 6

*Vary this recipe by using orange rind
and juice instead of lemon. Serve with
Sweet mousseline sauce (page 119). This
recipe is suitable for freezing.*

PREPARATION: About 15 minutes
COOKING: About 2 minutes
SETTING: Full power (100%)

3 (size 1) egg yolks
225 g/8 oz caster sugar
Finely grated rind of 2 large
   lemons, 325 g/12 oz total
   weight
3 tablespoons lemon juice,
   strained
3 tablespoons water
11 g/0.4 oz packet powdered
   gelatine

3 (size 1) egg whites, stiffly
whisked
150 ml/¼ pint double cream,
stiffly whipped, to decorate
4 pistachio nuts or a few
toasted flaked almonds

1 Prepare 6 individual ramekin
dishes. Make oiled greaseproof paper
collars round each dish to rise about
2.5 cm/1 inch above the rim. Hold
each in place with a rubber band or
string tied round the outside.
2 Place the egg yolks, sugar and
lemon rind in a medium bowl. Beat
together. Carefully follow these
instructions to avoid curdling the
eggs. (If overheated, they will cook
and coagulate.) Cook, uncovered, for
30 seconds, beat for 1 minute, cook
for 15 seconds, beat for 1 minute,
cook for 15 seconds, then beat for 3
minutes until thick and creamy.
3 Place the lemon juice and water in
a small jug. Cook, uncovered, for 1
minute or until boiling. Sprinkle the
gelatine powder over. Stir well until
dissolved. Gently pour into the egg
mixture, beating all the time. Leave
to cool.
4 Gently fold in the double cream,
then the egg whites.
5 Spoon the mixture into the
prepared ramekin dishes and
refrigerate until set.
6 Gently remove the greaseproof
paper collars and decorate each with
whipped cream and a pistachio nut.
Freezing: Use within 6 months.
Thawing: Thaw at room temperature
for about 2 hours.

ALMOND AND APPLE PANCAKES
For 4 to 5

*These can be served hot or cold, on
their own, or with a Cherry sauce (page
120) or a Sweet red wine sauce (page
121). The pancakes can be frozen.*

PREPARATION: About 10 minutes,
plus standing time for the batter
COOKING: About 4 minutes, plus
time to cook the pancakes
conventionally – on the hob, plus
refrigeration
SETTING: Full power (100%)

PANCAKES
125 g/4 oz plain flour
300 ml/½ pint milk
1 (size 1) egg
1 egg yolk
A pinch of salt
Oil for conventional frying
1 to 2 tablespoons sifted icing
sugar, to decorate

FILLING
A pinch of ground nutmeg
1 tablespoon brown sugar
450 g/1 lb dessert apples, peeled,
cored and thinly sliced
1 tablespoon orange juice
25 g/1 oz ground almonds
25 g/1 oz sultanas

1 To make the pancakes: Put the
flour into a bowl. Whisk together the
milk, egg, egg yolk and salt. Beat the
milk mixture into the flour until
smooth and free from lumps. Leave
to stand for 30 minutes.
2 Pour a little oil into a 20-cm/8-inch
frying pan. Heat and then spread 2
to 3 tablespoons of batter mixture
over the base of the frying pan. Cook
the pancake until it is nicely brown
and the top of the mixture is
bubbling. Turn it over and cook the
other side until brown. Chill, or keep
warm if serving hot. Repeat the
process until 4 or 5 pancakes have
been cooked.
3 To make the filling: Put the
nutmeg, sugar, apples and orange
juice in a medium bowl. Cook,
covered, for 4 minutes or until the
apples are tender. If you like the
apples very smooth, put the mixture
through a liquidiser or food processor.
Mix in the almonds and sultanas.
Chill in a refrigerator, or keep warm.

4 Fold each pancake in half, then half again. Fill each pocket with a spoonful of fruit mixture, making sure that it is well filled towards the point. (To serve hot, arrange on a serving dish and cook, uncovered, on Full power for 1 minute, or until heated through.)
5 Sift a little icing sugar over each pancake.
Freezing: Freeze after step 4. Use within 6 months.
Thawing: Full power (100%). Arrange the pancakes on a large round plate with the points of the pancake 'pockets' facing towards the outside of the plate. Cook, uncovered, for 2 minutes, turning the pancakes over halfway through cooking. Stand at room temperature for 20 minutes or until thawed. If serving cold, sift a little icing sugar over each. If serving hot, reheat, uncovered, as above, for 2 minutes or until warmed through. Then sift icing sugar over each.

SUMMER PUDDING
For 4

Although associated with warm summer days, this chilled pudding can be served all the year round. For those who find Christmas pudding too heavy, serve this – with a light Sweet mousseline sauce (page 119).

PREPARATION: About 15 minutes, plus refrigeration 24 hours
COOKING: About 7 minutes
SETTING: Full power (100%)

250 g/8 oz plums (unstoned weight), stones removed
125 g/4 oz strawberries, halved

125 g/4 oz raspberries
125 g/4 blackberries
125 g/4 oz caster sugar
1 tablespoon unsweetened orange juice
Rind of ½ an orange, finely grated
9 to 10 slices of white bread, crusts removed, each about 5 mm/¼ inch thick
150 ml/¼ pint double or whipping cream, to decorate

1 Place the plums, strawberries, raspberries, blackberries, sugar, orange juice and rind in a medium bowl. Cook, covered, for 7 minutes or until the plums are tender.
2 Meanwhile, line a 1.2-litre/2-pint pudding basin with the bread, making sure by overlapping each slice that the base and sides are covered and there are no gaps. Keep enough bread aside to cover the top of the fruit mixture.
3 Use a slotted spoon to transfer the cooked fruit into the basin. Cover with the remaining bread and spoon the juice over the pudding. Keep any extra juice in a covered jug in the refrigerator.
4 Place a small plate or saucer on the top of the bread and then a heavy weight on top of the plate or saucer. If you have no weight, place a bag of sugar in a plastic bag to keep the sugar dry and use this. Refrigerate for 24 hours.
5 Gently loosen the pudding and turn it out on to a chilled plate. Slowly spoon over the remaining juice, making sure that all the bread is coloured.
6 Decorate with whipped cream.

Freezing: Freeze after step 5. Use within 6 months.

Thawing: Full power (100%). Stand on a plate. Cook, covered, for 3 minutes. Turn the pudding into a 1.2-litre/2-pint pudding basin. Cook, covered, for 1½ minutes. Stand for 40 minutes or until thawed. Turn out on to a chilled plate. Continue at step 6.

COFFEE ICE CREAM BOMBE
For 4

This delicious ice cream is very rich. It could be served with a Butterscotch sauce (page 121).

PREPARATION: About 15 minutes, plus freezing time
COOKING: About 7 minutes, plus 10 minutes standing time
SETTING: Full power (100%)

300 ml/½ pint milk
1 (size 1) egg
2 (size 2) egg yolks
2 tablespoons coffee essence
300 ml/½ pint double cream
150 ml/¼ pint double or whipping cream, whipped, to decorate

1 Pour the milk into a small jug. Cook, uncovered, for 3 minutes or until boiling. Set aside for 10 minutes.
2 Place the egg and yolks in a bowl, and beat together until creamy and pale. Stir in the milk and coffee essence. Strain into a large jug.
3 Cook, uncovered, for 4 minutes or until the custard lightly coats the back of a wooden spoon. Beat every minute to avoid curdling. Beat well before setting aside to cool. Whisk occasionally during cooling.
4 Whisk the double cream until thick and fold it into the cooled egg custard. Pour into a bowl and freeze until partially frozen, about an hour.
5 Remove the ice cream from the freezer and whisk until smooth. Pour into a 900–ml/1½–pint cream bombe mould or basin and freeze until solid.
6 Remove from the freezer 15 to 20 minutes before serving. Turn out on to a chilled plate and decorate with cream.
Freezing: Use within 2 months.
Thawing: See step 6.

BLACKCURRANT SORBET
For 4

Serve the sorbet as a dessert or after a spicy starter to clear the palate before the main course. Any favourite fruit juice can be used instead of the blackcurrant juice.

PREPARATION: About 10 minutes, plus refrigeration
COOKING: About 4 minutes
SETTING: Full power (100%)

900 ml/1½ pint blackcurrant juice
2 rounded teaspoons powdered gelatine
150 g/5 oz granulated sugar
2 egg whites (size 1), stiffly whisked

1 Pour 300 ml/½ pint blackcurrant juice into a large jug. Stir in the gelatine and sugar. Cook, uncovered, for 4 minutes or until the sugar has dissolved, stirring halfway through cooking.
2 Stir well, then stir in the remaining juice. Pour into a large bowl. Freeze until the edges of the mixture begin to set.
3 Whisk the mixture until thick, then whisk in the egg whites. Freeze until frozen solid.
4 Remove from the freezer and refrigerate for 15 minutes before serving. This softens the sorbet to a pleasant – not rock-hard – texture.
Freezing: Use within 6 months.
Thawing: See step 4.

Index

133

COLLECT THE

other books in this series:

A complete recipe library

Notes

Notes

Notes

Notes

Notes

Notes

Notes